PASTORALISTS
OF THE ANDES

The Alpaca Herders of Paratía

PASTORALISTS OF THE ANDES

The Alpaca Herders of Paratía

Jorge A. Flores-Ochoa
Ralph Bolton, *translator*

 A Publication of the
Institute for the Study of Human Issues
Philadelphia

Manufactured in the United States of America

Library of Congress Cataloging in Publication Data:

Flores-Ochoa, Jorge A
   Pastoralists of the Andes.

   Translation of Los pastores de Paratía.
   Bibliography: p.
   Includes index.
   1. Indians of South America—Peru—Paratia—Social life and customs. 2. Paratia, Peru—Social life and customs. I. Title.
F3429.1.P25F5713   301.29′85′3   78–31360
ISBN 0–915980–89–4

For information, write:

Director of Publications
ISHI
3401 Science Center
Philadelphia, Pennsylvania 19104
U.S.A.

To my mother with filial love.
To Gustavo Aníbal and Miguel Ángel with hope.

All the herders respected and offered sacrifices to the [constellation] astrologers know as Lyra. The herders called it *Urcuchillay* and said it was a sheep [llama] of many colors, responsible for the preservation of the livestock. Its feet and head were formed from small stars below, in the shape of a T. Close to it is another formation they worshipped, called *Catachillay,* also quite large, and a smaller one nearby. These they said were a llama with its offspring who descended from *Urcuchillay*. / *Cobo 1956 [1653]: 159*

CONTENTS

ILLUSTRATIONS

OVER A PERIOD of several thousand years, humans have successfully adapted to the difficult environmental conditions found at extremely high altitudes in the Andes. The unique pattern of stresses and resources associated with this ecological setting has stimulated biological and cultural responses that have permitted humans to inhabit remote regions as high as 4,700 meters above sea level. For most Peruvian highlanders, adaptation has included the development of a sophisticated subsistence system based on the production of corn, potatoes, and native cereals such as *kinuwa* and *kaniwa*. Since the upper limit of cultivation for most Andean tubers and grains is 4,250 meters, survival at higher altitudes requires different subsistence strategies. In such areas, scattered throughout the Central Andes, people rely on herds of alpacas and llamas for their livelihood. This volume by Jorge A. Flores-Ochoa presents a description of the culture of Paratía, a community of alpaca herdsmen in southern Peru.

Dr. Flores-Ochoa's book on Paratía was published in Spanish in 1968. During the following decade, his work on Andean pastoralism achieved recognition as a major contribution to the ethnography of the region. Although a fair amount of research has been done on Andean agricultural communities, very little was known about Andean pastoralists prior to the publication of Dr. Flores-Ochoa's account.

This book is important, however, not only as an addition to the understanding of the diversity of cultures existing in the Andes, but also as a significant contribution to the anthropological literature on pastoral societies. It has generally been assumed by scholars interested in pastoralism that herding as a

1

dominant subsistence strategy emerged *only* in the Old World, where, to be sure, pastoralism is prominent and well documented in such places as the Middle East, East Africa, Central Asia, and northern Scandinavia. Further, it is often assumed that the only true pastoralists in the New World are the Navajo, whose pastoral activities developed as a result of the introduction of sheep after the conquest of the Americas by Europeans. Professor Flores-Ochoa's work raises serious questions about these assumptions. The community he describes is probably as exclusively pastoral as any group elsewhere in the world, and there is some evidence suggesting that this subsistence mode may be ancient in the Andes.

Contemporary pastoralists, regardless of location, are under strong assimilative pressures. Traditional pastoral cultures are being transformed at a rapid pace: see, for example, the case of the Same (Lapps) of northern Finland described by Pertti Pelto in *The Snowmobile Revolution* (Cummings, 1973). Technological developments, the extension of communications networks, the growth of national and international markets, agrarian reform, and other processes have placed many pastoral groups in a precarious position. Andean pastoralists have not escaped influences that are likely to destroy their present way of life. It is fortunate that Dr. Flores-Ochoa was able to study the culture of Paratía before it was greatly altered. Following his work in Paratía, he conducted additional research on other herding communities, and recently edited a volume containing numerous articles on Andean pastoralism (*Pastores de puna, uywamichiq punarunakuna*, Institute of Peruvian Studies, 1977). Readers who wish to pursue the topic further should consult this edited volume, which contains an excellent bibliography on Andean pastoralism, although most of the articles are currently available only in Spanish.

The present book is a translation of a slightly modified version of *Los pastores de Paratía*. This edition, for example, contains a chart showing the cycle of pastoral activities in Paratía, as well as some footnotes and clarifications within the text that did not appear in the original. These changes have been introduced at the author's request. New photographs have been added, principally from the collection of Dr. Flores-Ochoa; the captions are my own, though they are often based on Dr. Flores-Ochoa's notations.

Thanks are due to the Inter-American Indian Institute for granting permission to publish this translation. I would like to express my gratitude, too, to the following persons who collaborated on this project: Melinda Collins, who helped with a draft of one chapter; Wayne Lim, who read and commented on an early draft of the translation; Corinne Bybee, who patiently typed and retyped the manuscript; and Charlene Bolton, who prepared an index for the book. Finally, I am indebted to Douglas Gordon and the ISHI staff for their painstaking efforts to improve my prose: without their careful editing the reader might have been amused but not enlightened by my attempt to retain the charming style of the Spanish version.

Ralph Bolton

AUTHOR'S
ACKNOWLEDGMENTS

MANY PEOPLE helped me in diverse ways with the preparation of this book, offering selfless and gracious assistance. Among them, I would like to acknowledge the contributions of Dr. John H. Rowe, who kindly read several sections, providing valuable criticisms and suggestions; Dr. Patricia Lyon, my former teacher, who read and commented on the entire manuscript; Dr. Oscar Núñez del Prado Castro, with whom I consulted about several topics discussed in this work; Dr. Manuel Chávez Ballon, who generously provided me with a map of the Paratía region; and especially Dr. John V. Murra, who encouraged me in the preparation of a revised version of my original manuscript and devoted valuable time to checking, analyzing, and criticizing the work so that it could be published by the Inter-American Indian Institute. Many suggestions made by these scholars could not be incorporated in this account because of the insufficiency or absence of pertinent data; we hope to remedy this at some future time. For the help they gave me in Paratía, I am deeply indebted to Mr. Enrique Vizcarra and his wife, Mrs. Asunta Guevara de Vizcarra, whose knowledge of the area and its culture greatly facilitated my work.

Although I do not deserve the credit for all that is accurate and worthwhile in this work, I alone am responsible for any remaining errors, defects, gaps, omissions, and points subject to debate, correction, or clarification.

I must stress the role played by Dr. Vladimiro Bermejo Quiroga, Director in 1964 of the Institute of Socio-Economic Studies of the Technical University of the Altiplano in Puno, Peru, which sponsored my work. His tremendous enthusiasm and vision aided my research in Paratía. Likewise, this project would not have been possible without the facilities and support given by the present rector of the Technical University of the Altiplano, Ing. Alberto Barreda.

Preparation of the present manuscript for publication was carried out while I was in the United States on a grant from the Ford Foundation.

To all the above, my sincere thanks, and to the people of Paratía, my eternal gratitude.

AUTHOR'S PREFACE
TO THE SPANISH EDITION

IN THE SECOND CHAPTER of this book we shall refer to the *ayarachi*, a very impressive musical ensemble renowned as much for the costumes worn by its members as for the musical harmony of their instruments, panpipes called *zampoñas*. For many, the *ayarachi* is synonymous with Paratía and vice versa. But, as we shall try to demonstrate, Paratía encompasses much more than simply *ayarachi* ensembles.

In 1964 the author was a professor in the Department of Anthropology at the Institute of Socio-Economic Studies of the Technical University of the Altiplano in the city of Puno. Thanks to the support of Dr. Vladimiro Bermejo Quiroga, Director of the Institute, it was possible to plan a project of field investigation to gather ethnographic material. After a reconnaissance trip, Paratía was chosen. There it was possible to document the existence of human groups whose subsistence is based on alpaca herding, supplemented with income from textile production and commerce. Serious gaps exist in the anthropological literature concerning Andean pastoralism, and claims have been made which are contradicted or weakened by the material gathered during this investigation.

Since we intend to talk about herders and a pastoral community which fits into what Aguirre Beltrán (1967) calls "refuge regions," we should make clear just what it is that we refer to as "pastoralism." Let us look at two simple conceptual definitions:

Pastoralism: An economic system in which production from or with domesticated animals constitutes a major economic resource. [Jacobs and Stern 1964:319]

Pastoralism: An economy that derives the bulk of the food supply from domesticated animals. Pastoralists usually do not eat plant products, except those obtained by trading or gathering. They often travel or migrate to get good pastures, and there is sometimes conflict between pastoralists and farmers. The animals may provide milk, meat, transport, hides, and hair. [Winick 1961:403]

Pastoral societies, then, are ones that use their flocks as their means of subsistence, or exchange animal products for crops grown by neighboring farmers. Of course we should also take into account the *emphasis* the society places on animal husbandry—the emotions that such an occupation arouses. Paratía clearly meets the first criterion. As for the second, we will see that animal husbandry is a concern of great social importance, surrounded by religious ceremony; it is a cultural focus in Paratía for both men and women.

This report, which does not pretend to be anything but an introduction to the topic, has been divided into four chapters. The first three are devoted to descriptions of the natural environment, the culture, and the economy, and the fourth to a brief discussion of the possibility of the existence of pure pastoralism as a cultural manifestation in the central Andes.

We have not included detailed demographic data from the records of the District Council of Paratía because such information is not directly related to the central focus of this book. Nor is a sketch of the town included because, unfortunately, we lost the one we had made and there was no means of obtaining another.

Quechua words have been written according to the orthographic guidelines established by the Third Inter-American Indian Congress of La Paz, Bolivia, in 1954. At the same time, we have attempted as closely as possible to record the local Quechua dialect as it is spoken in Paratía. Sometimes we use the letter "j" for aspirated sounds, as in the word *llijlla* (carrying cloth).

When the words "indigenous," "*cholo*," and "mestizo" are used, we try to confine them to the definitions established by Mangin (1964), Bourricaud (1954, 1963, and 1967), Núñez del Prado (1953), and the *Regional Development Plan for Southern Peru* (see Plan Regional 1959).

Complete bibliographical references are found at the end of the book. Following the method created by Dr. John H. Rowe, numbers between brackets [ ] indicate the date of the first edition of a publication.

Ethnographic field work was carried out in July and August of 1964, after a preliminary trip in June. A follow-up visit took place in October, during which we were accompanied by Dr. Máximo Neyra Avendaño, an archeologist from the National University of Arequipa under contract to the Technical University of the Altiplano. In this short time, it was possible to record only the most salient aspects of the culture. We hope to return for a longer period to continue this work and to join the herders on their journeys through the Andean cordillera.

Jorge A. Flores-Ochoa

PASTORALISTS
OF THE ANDES

The Alpaca Herders of Paratía

CHAPTER 1

PUNA, ICHU GRASS, AND ALPACAS

SURROUNDED BY the imposing landscape of the Western Cordillera of the central Andes in South America, at the foot of high, massive mountain peaks, many of which are always covered with snow, is an area of great ethnographic interest. Called Paratía, it is found in the province of Lampa, in the department of Puno, in the southern part of Peru, between 70°12' and 70°44' longitude and 15°12' and 15°44' latitude.

Along the Qomer River

The settlement of Paratía, capital of the district with the same name, is reached by a dusty trail which is accessible on a regular basis only during the dry season, from April to October or November. During the rest of the year, the summer or rainy season, the road often becomes impassable to motor vehicles because of deep mud puddles and quagmires. Nor can one reach Paratía when the waters of the Qomer River rise; there is no bridge, and the river cannot be crossed without danger.*

The road, one of the main ones leading to Paratía, begins at Santa Lucía, 4,083 meters above sea level. This small town in the department of Puno is on the rail line that provides

---

*According to reports, the construction of a bridge over the Qomer River was finished in 1965.

Map 1.   Paratía, in the Department of Puno

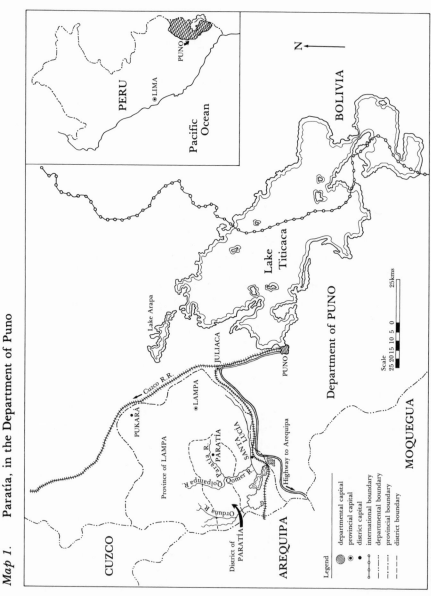

service between Cuzco, Puno, and Arequipa. Starting from the north side of town, the road follows a course parallel to the Qomer River for approximately fifty kilometers until the Qomer meets the Paratía River. From there the road continues along the shore of this river, for which the district is named.

Along the way, the road passes through several hacienda settlements, such as Choroma and Alpakoyo, and through many Indian hamlets. There is no scheduled means of transportation between Paratía and Santa Lucía. The only vehicles that arrive in Paratía are those transporting cargo and passengers for traditional fiestas or carrying government officials who occasionally travel there for administrative reasons. These officials might be from the Regional Health Agency (*Área de Salud*), the Puno Development Corporation (CORPUNO), the Ministry of Agriculture, the Mining Administration (*Dirección de Minería*), or the Farm Bank (*Banco Agropecuario*). The vehicles and their occupants are objects of curiosity for the few residents who chance to be in the vicinity.

Another access route unites the district with the provincial capital of Lampa: a trail used by travelers on foot, horseback riders, and llama drivers. Approximately forty-five kilometers long, with abrupt ascents and steep slopes, it can be traveled in a day. This route is the one most commonly used because Lampa is the town where most of the public services available to the people of Paratía are located, and where administrative, judicial, and other transactions must be carried out. The Santa Lucía route is seldom used because it requires motor vehicles and is almost triple the distance of the trail to Lampa.

A highway to Lampa, following more or less the route of the trail, is under construction. This is a project cherished by many Paratía mestizos. However, the completion of this road will take time because of a shortage of funds and the extremely rocky terrain. Countless paths which meander along the slopes of the mountains and crisscross the undulations of the puna, or plateau, are used for travel between hamlets and among homesteads (*anexos, caseríos,* and *estancias*).

The District

According to a law passed by the Peruvian Congress, Paratía is considered a district. But the ethnographic zone to which this book refers does not coincide precisely with the district boundaries established by the law; rather, the zone extends beyond those boundaries in several places. The northern border of the district follows a line from the snow-capped peak of Qiles in a northeasterly direction along the watershed that forms the northern drainage area of the Qeyesaña, Saqene, Sayto, and Paratía rivers, crossing the mountains called Qilqa, Hatumpasto, San Luis, Mina, Fieldoymina, and Sobrerura. The eastern boundary follows the watershed which separates the countryside of Lampa and Cabanillas from the Paratía River to the south; reference points along the way are the summits of Mts. Warayapunta, Papana, Caballuna, Sakamanapunta, and Agullana. In the south the boundary travels in a westerly direction along the divide separating the basin of the Paratía River from the watershed of the Serpuntana and Kashina rivers, passing the summits of Kondorini and Quiere to emerge beyond the basin of the Qolpampa River. There, in the west, it meets the stream that descends from Mt. Soñapata near the settlement of Wanatiri. The line continues in the west along the divide between the Kollpamayo and Orduña rivers, passing through the crests of Takllok and Qinsamita. Then it proceeds to the northeast, along the divide separating the waters of the Qolpampa River basin from those which enter the Orduña River, to Amanda Lake and the Palaquina River. After passing the crest of Kuycha mountain, and the northern sector of the Ankasi and the Koñamiri, the boundary line once again touches the snowy summit of Qilqa.

Politically, the district contains several *parcialidades* (communities): in the west, Chawpiwayta; in the east, Chanawayta; in the north, Koarita; in the southeast, Harpaña; in the southwest, Chingani; and of course the village of Paratía itself. It is interesting to note that the law creating the district in some cases considers simple huts or compounds, many of them only two or three one-roomed huts, as hamlets. These hamlets—

Map 2. The District of Paratía

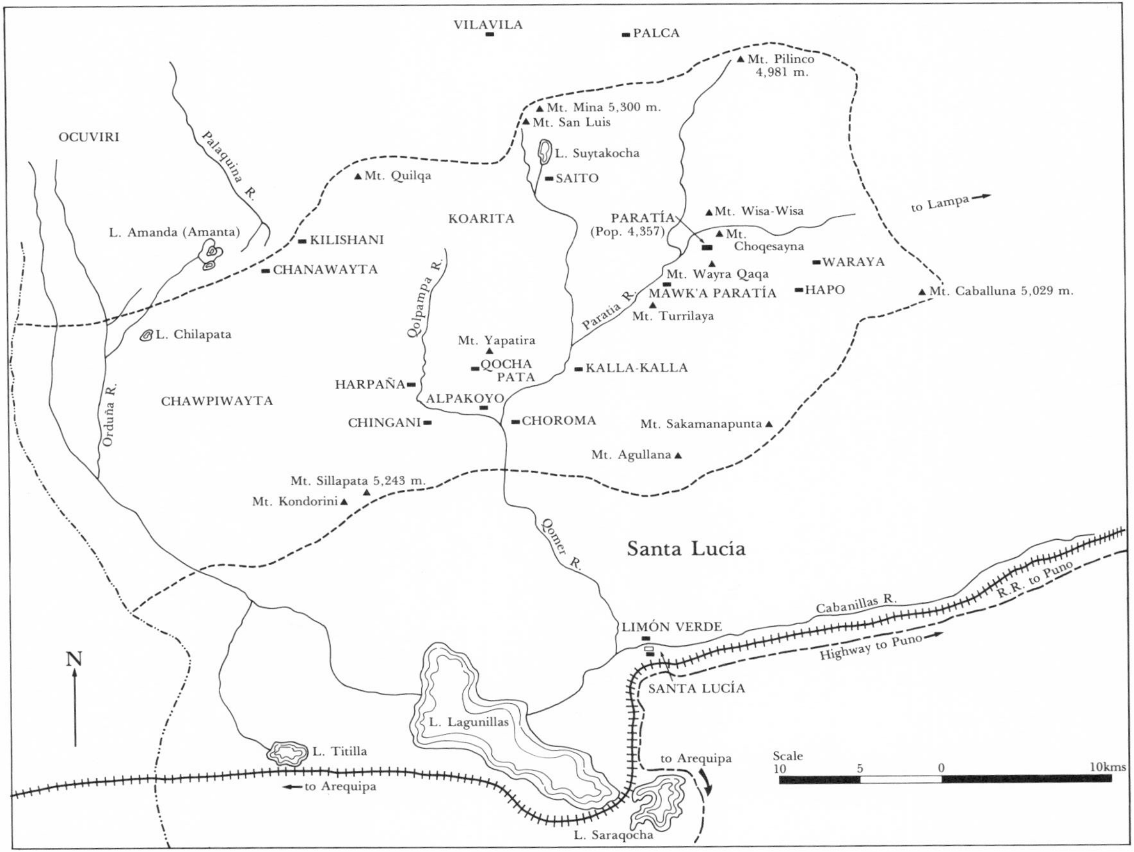

including Chanawayta, Chingani, Waraya, San Antonio, Alpakoyo, San José de Makalaka, Harpaña, Pakaje, Sora, and Hapo—were all withdrawn from the districts of Lampa, Santa Lucía, and Pukará when the district of Paratía was established.

The Puna

The average altitude of the area is more than 4,300 meters above sea level, although some of the mountain peaks reach 5,243 meters and more, as in the case of Mount Sillapata. According to the ecological classification found in the *Regional Development Plan for Southern Peru* (Plan Regional 1959), Paratía corresponds to the puna subregion—whose formations include tundra, alpine, and subalpine barren plain—although some of its higher reaches correspond to the nival ecological formation.

Altitude can be considered the main factor in the area's cold, subhumid climate, in which the average temperature fluctuates between 5 and 10 degrees centigrade (Plan Regional 1959). Daily temperature variations are very pronounced, with much sun and even warmth during the daytime, followed by afternoons which quickly turn cold as soon as the sun begins to set. Temperature changes are brusque, and the thermometer may descend 15 to 20 degrees in less than three hours, going below the freezing point even while the last rays of the sun can still be seen. Frosts can occur during any season of the year, but they are more frequent and severe between May and August.

The rains, which begin in sporadic fashion in October and increase during November, intensify at the end of December and last until the final days of March or the beginning of April. Snowfalls vary in depth and can occur at any time of the year, but they are more common in the summer, the rainy season. At that time snow may cover the ground with layers several centimeters thick. On many days, one can see only the whiteness of the snow contrasting with the deep blue of the sky.

At any hour of the day, but especially in the afternoon, strong winds blow, most of them from east to west. Around the mountain passes and peaks the winds are often very strong. The most powerful and feared is known as *phuku,* a wind of the high outback which, according to local traditions, is capable of lifting a horseman off his mount and throwing him to the ground. Most often the *phuku* is accompanied by snow, producing blizzards with blinding whirlwinds. The *phuku,* as the natives wisely say, penetrates the body, even "to a depth where the sun does not reach." Another strong wind which rumbles among the peaks of the cordillera and through the rocky outcroppings is the famous *wayna q'ajcha wayra.* The natives report that this awesome wind can dislocate a person's lower jaw, fling the roofs of houses to the ground, and break cliffs into boulders, at the same time sending out terrifying bellows and roars. There are those who swear that the *tutukas wayra,* another name by which this wind is known, is even capable of killing people.

In general terms, the landscape is extremely wild and captivating. Because of the luminosity at this high altitude, the mountain peaks seem to be right at one's fingertips, but they move back into the distance when one tries to approach them. Flat areas are small, while undulating terrain extends for kilometers. Vegetation is of the microthermic type, with an absence of trees that is characteristic of steppes. In summer the fields are yellowish with light streaks of green that reveal the presence of streams, springs, and marshy places. When the rains begin, the pastures take on a greenish color which slowly intensifies as the downpours continue. When snow falls, the scene is marvelous. Against the white background the natives are silhouetted in their colorful dress, whistling and shouting as they drive their herds of llamas.

The soil is characteristic of highlands with undulant or rough slopes and freezing rocky areas. Grazing areas are surrounded by steep mountains. Most of the soil, according to the *Regional Development Plan for Southern Peru* (Plan Regional 1959), has a marked degree of acidity, ranging from moderate to very strong. Its basic components come principally from a great variety of sedimentary volcanic rocks. One can also detect the presence of limestone in the soil. Soil fertility, which is

An undulating landscape is characteristic of Paratía and other zones in southern Peru where alpaca herding is important. Interrupted in places by high mountain peaks, treeless and windswept, the terrain looks rugged and compelling. Dispersed over this vast area are the huts or *cabañas* used by the pastoralists for shelter while tending their herds in the uplands during the summer season. In the corral shown here is a *pikota*, a rock that serves as an altar when propitiatory rites are conducted associated with a high organic content, is low, as is the nitrogen content. The percentage of phosphorus is high. According to the study mentioned above, the main factors determining the composition of the soil are climate and vegetation.

Traveling across the countryside one notices the presence of ore crushers and adits, evidence of subsoil mining. The majority of these works have been abandoned, perhaps since the early years of the republican era or even the days of the viceroyalty. At present several mines are in operation, and once again minerals are being extracted from the abandoned galleries to the southwest of the town of Paratía. Piles of slag from former mines, today in ruins, are being exploited anew now that modern technology makes it possible to extract ore from these residues. Such is the case, for example, with the silver slag from Mawk'a Paratía, which is transported to the concentration plant at Limón Verde near Santa Lucía.

The mineral deposits originate in filled-in fractures of various sizes; the veins range from small lodes to thick ones several kilometers in length (Plan Regional 1959). In most cases, veins are of the filled-in fracture type, with a wealth of ruby silver near the surface diminishing in quantity at greater depths, where galena, sphalerite, and chalcopyrite increase. Many varieties of quartz are also present.

The strong and continuous winds seem to be the main cause of soil erosion, since at these altitudes the dryness of the winds is extreme; according to Quijada's observations quoted by Choy:

the high plains are razed more because of the strong air currents than because of the heat. Wind at a velocity of two meters per second evaporates a greater quantity of water from the soil in twenty-four hours than a day of intense sunlight. The temperature of the surface can vary from 50 to 60 degrees, and decline to 10°C below zero. [Choy 1960:167]

This is why in Paratía one can see large stretches of terrain, barren of all vegetation and soil, with rocks already exposed on the surface.

Rivers and Mountains

Since the area we are studying is in the heart of the cordillera, there are several snowy peaks where rapid streams of clear water begin. Some streams are sporadic while others are permanent. The principal hydrographic basins are the ones formed by the Paratía River, the Qomer River (which is also known as Río Verde or Green River), and the Orduña River, although the catchment areas of the Qeyesaña, Saqene, Sayto, Serpuntana, Kashina, Qolpampa, Kollpamayo, and Palaquina rivers are also important. Of the several lakes in the area we shall mention only Chilapata and Suytakocha. Mineral and thermal waters have also been reported in the region.

The highest and most impressive peaks within the borders of Paratía are Wisa-Wisa, Wayra Qaqa, Choqesayna, and Qayqo. Other no less notable mountains are the peaks of Qinsamita and Kuycha. From many summits, such as Awallo and Qiles, it is possible on clear sunny days to see in the distance the smoky peaks of volcanoes—Misti in the Arequipa and Ubinas in Moquequa. The silver sheen of Lake Titicaca is also visible.

Ichu Grass and Pastures

The Altiplano or "high plain" is often called the "zone without trees" and this description is well deserved. The vegetation of microthermic regions does not include arboreal forms. The flora is almost completely limited to small plants, with an abundance of the forage type necessary for herding—the tough grasses especially suited for lamoids (alpacas, llamas, and vicuñas), which in certain instances are the only animals capable of digesting them.

The most important types of grasses are *champa pasto* (*Muhlenbergia legularis*) and *rama pasto* (*Calamagrostis* sp.), the favorites of the alpacas. There is also a great variety of straw plants, including *ichu* (*Stepis* sp.) and *chilliwa* (*Festuca dolicophylla*), and cactaceous plants, such as the *sankayo* (*Opuntia* sp.)—whose beautiful flowers are the source of inspiration for many *waynos,* or popular Andean songs—the *kiska (Opuntia* sp.), and the *kisa (Urtica* sp.). The *wallakaya* (unidentified), which grows in the highest mountains, is used, as are many other plants, in the practice of magic, and some plants, such as the *sallikata* (unidentified), are drunk in hot brews as matés or infusions. Mosses, lichens, and other forms of vegetation are abundant, perhaps in a greater number than one would imagine in such frigid land.

Some individuals struggle to raise more fragile plants, including trees such as the *kewña sacha (Polylepis* sp.), covering them with woolen blankets at night so the cold will not freeze the sap or the dawn sun crack the stalk.*

Alpacas and Other Animals

Although the fauna is varied, especially the small animals, the most important and familiar local animals are the large ruminant mammals domesticated by the ancient Peruvians.

It is worth mentioning, since many people believe it to be impossible, that in Paratía there is a type of large, black fly equipped with an enormous stinger that it uses to attack men and animals. The *chichiranka,* as they are called, abound between May and November and are very annoying, especially on sunny days. With the first rains, the *chichiranka* begin to disappear, as a new stage in their life cycle develops. There are also several varieties of butterflies—the most common and best known of which is the yellow-winged *frailita* (unidentified)—and spiders of several sizes and colors.

Frogs and toads can be found in the rivers and streams, as well as the marshes and swamps. Large rocks are the preferred habitat of the *kalaywa,* or lizards *(Tropidorus peruviana),* which select warm boulders for sunning themselves.

The sky is filled with a host of birds in many colors; we can mention but a few. Around the numerous lagoons and natural

---

*Scientific names have been taken from Herrera (1918, 1921, and 1934), Pulgar (1946), Sauer (1950), Towle (1961), and Marín (1961).

ponds, ducks, *qhan-qhan* (*Anas* sp.), and *qeweyllo* (unidentified) are commonly seen. The *qeweyllo* is white and resembles the sea gull; another similar bird is the *killwa* (*Larus serranus*). Needless to say, sea gulls and *wallatas* (*Chleophaga melanoptera*) are not lacking. Another aquatic bird, the *p'aksilla* (unidentified), is a lovely gray color. Other birds include the *ch'iti* (unidentified); the *hakakllu* (*Colaptes puna*); the *leqe-leqe* or *leqechu* (*Ptilescelys resplendes*); the *papachiku* (unidentified), which greatly resembles the sparrow and, according to the natives, is "more nutritious than ten sheep put together"; the *pisaka* or partridge (*Ptyomura albifrontis*); the *kivio*, a bird larger than the partridge, with a tasty meat; and the *qello-pesqo* (unidentified), a yellow bird with a bluish head, also called *para pesqo,* or "rain bird," because it flies in a harried and rapid way, forming groups when it senses the coming of rain. Flying majestically in the upper altitudes is the condor (*Vultur gryphus*), the king of these heights. In a few homesteads there are common domesticated chickens of undefined breed (Pulgar 1946; Gilmore 1950; and Dr. Ángel Flores Bustamante, personal communication).

In the waters of the Paratía and Qomer rivers, as in those of the Orduña and other minor streams, it is possible to find trout (Plan Regional 1959). They were introduced by the Peruvian government, which began to introduce young fish in Lake Titicaca and some highland rivers in 1946. Over the years, the trout have flourished and now inhabit most of the waterways in the department of Puno. The varieties found here are the rainbow trout (*Salmo irideus*) and river trout (*Salmo fario*). There are those who insist that they have caught specimens up to half a meter long.

On the hillsides, competing for the scarce pasture with the lamoids, are countless viscacha (*Lagidium peruanum*), a burrowing South American rodent. In remote places that men cannot easily reach, pumas establish their lairs. Accustomed to attacking herds, especially those with small animals, the pumas (*Felis concolor*) are a source of worry for herders. Dangerous to a lesser degree are the *oskhollo* (*Felis pajerus*). There are many foxes (*Ducycion inca*), and living peacefully with them are the skunks, *añas* or *zorrinos* (*Conepatos inca*). A few households raise

The pastoralist's way of life in Paratía is based on his herd of alpacas. These animals provide him with most of the materials he needs to survive. Alpacas are tranquil animals; they can be tended by any member of the family, including young children. Each morning the alpacas must be taken out to pasture and each afternoon they must be brought back to the corrals surrounding the homestead. An alpaca herd is colorful since the coats of the animals occur in a large variety of hues, especially black, white, gray, and many shades of brown.

guinea pigs called *kuwis* (*Vicia cobaya*), which are of lesser importance here than at lower altitudes.

The most important animal in this region is the alpaca (*Lama pacos*), since, as this work will demonstrate, human social development is possible at these altitudes in large measure because of these animals. Many important aspects of the culture revolve around or are related to the alpaca, its care, and the products it yields. The alpaca and the llama (*Lama glama*), mammals native to the highlands, were domesticated by pre-Columbian man in the Andes. On the most remote and highest peaks, far from the predatory reach of the *misti*, or mestizo, one sometimes sees isolated specimens of the beautiful and slender vicuñas (*Lama vicugna*) (Pulgar 1946; Gilmore 1950; Dr. Ángel Flores Bustamante, personal communication). Numerous herds of magnificent animals once grazed on the hillsides. Now they have become a memory, the subject of nostalgic stories told by men forty or fifty or older. The mestizos, with their greed and their automatic weapons, did not hesitate to destroy an entire herd of vicuñas in a day in order to acquire and sell the extremely fine wool.

In some areas, especially in the lower plateau, there are flocks of sheep, a few cows, and even fewer horses. All the compounds have ferocious dogs, their hair blown into tangles by the wind.

Gentiles and Miners

Many of the problems in this research could have been precluded if we had historical information and documentation, but for a variety of reasons we could not obtain it. Nonetheless, we believe this gap will eventually be remedied and would like to encourage others to pursue the task. Perhaps with an audacity that exceeds the depth of our data, we will still make some comments of a general nature.

People in Paratía suggest that there are years when the amount of rain reaches alarming levels and the snowfalls are heavier than usual. According to the natives, these snowfalls are responsible for the name of their homeland. They tell us that "Paratía" is derived from the Quechua word *Paraqtiyanan,* which means "where the rain resides." They add that the noun *para* does not refer exactly to rain, but rather to snow since raindrops fall violently, while snowflakes descend gently.

Although this etymology is preferred locally, the name may have Aymara roots. Bertonio (1612:250, 353) lists the following:

> *Para:* Forehead; *Yauripara,* shameless, impudent.
> *Paraña: uel Para Haqese:* one with a big forehead.
> *Ti:* a particle that is used very much in interrogative sentences, and for adornment in negatives, and rarely is left off when needed. . . . *Tiana:* seat of bundled totora.

Human occupation prior to the arrival of the European invaders might be inferred from the existence of *gentiles,* the name given in the region to pre-Columbian burial sites and in general to all places where there are mummified human remains. The remains themselves are also called *gentiles,* and everything associated with them is considered the property or activity of the *gentiles.** Cemeteries of this kind are said to exist in Turrilaya, Puruwayqo, Salkoyo, Kiswarani, Tumaruma, Champikancha, Chawpiwayta, Mollota, Okhu, and many other places. There is also a profusion of caverns and rocky refuges in the area. It would be by no means strange to discover that many of them were used in the remote past. It would be safe to assume that the human remains buried in tombs built in the cliffs and escarpments belong to inhabitants of pre-Columbian eras. But the existence of early human occupation is only a possibility. It must be confirmed or dismissed with archeological evidence; conceivably, one might find preceramic sites.

Since the land is rich in metals, especially silver-bearing ones, it would have awakened the greed of the Spaniards who explored it, traveled through it, and succeeded in establishing themselves in a more or less permanent way. They left behind quite a few traces of their activity, the most prominent of which are on the shores of the Kashina River. There one finds the ruins of buildings, probably mills and metal foundries, in addition to many houses presumably intended for the miners.

However, the major site seems to be the one known in Quechua as Mawk'a Paratía (in Spanish, Antigua Paratía; in English, Old Paratía), located approximately four kilometers from the present capital town of the district. There one can see clearly the remains of old buildings of unworked stone, put together with a mortar of clay and lime. One can still make out the ruins of the chapel, the refinery, the foundations of the foundry, the great central patio surrounded by one-story rooms, and the gabled walls over which the roof beams were laid. The central courtyard is crossed by a narrow channel branching off from a larger one that conveyed water to the

---

*The term has roughly the same meaning as the English word "gentiles" when it is used to mean "pagans." [Trans.]

mill. It might have supplied water for domestic consumption as well as for the watering trough of the animals used in the mines. The central courtyard had a main entrance with a door that could be locked from inside, as shown by the openings in the wall where the crossbar was inserted. Near the chapel are large rooms that served as storehouses or dormitories. Scattered about the entire site are many thick ceramic fragments of colonial origin—mostly, it would seem, remnants of pots with conical bases. Finally, the abandoned millstones can still be seen. Certainly this is an ideal place to carry out research in colonial archeology.

The relocation of Paratía to its present site was effected at some undetermined time, probably at the beginning of the second half of the last century. The main reason for this change might have been the need to be closer to the new mines, above all the very rich silver mines in the hill called Wayra Qaqa ("Windy Cliff"), on whose lower slopes the new Paratía was erected. But the move was also permeated with mysticism and legend, which perhaps were used by the Spaniards to cover their intentions and avoid feelings of uneasiness that could have led to other interpretations.

In Old Paratía, an image of the Virgin of Bethlehem was the object of veneration. On many mornings, the faithful who went to worship in the small chapel would not find the Virgin in her niche. After a search, she was always found in a place called Pakla Pata and taken back to the altar. Time after time she would vanish during the night, or appear in the morning with her dress dirty and her feet covered with dust and mud, having soiled them while walking through the fields at night. These events were interpreted as an expression of the divine desire for a new chapel to be built in the place where the image was found. For this reason, a new house of worship was built, around which the present town of Paratía was constructed. One can still see two or three houses in ruins with clear evidence of old construction. Tradition states that the mine near the new site of Paratía yielded huge quantities of precious metal but was abandoned because of a terrible tragedy. Nearly fifty miners were trapped by a landslide in one of the galleries, and their bodies were never recovered for Christian burial. That is why today on certain nights it is still possible to hear the cries and laments of their ghostly souls.

In a list of parishes published in 1905, Paratía appears as a vice-parish of Lampa under the name "Paratic Lampa" (Sanmartí 1905:258). This could be an error because there is no oral memory of the name. As a vice-district, Paratía was an integral part of the district of Lampa, capital of the province of the same name. It included the *parcialidades* of Chawpiwayta, Chanawayta, Hatun Ayllu, Chingani, and Harpaña, each of which had a governor. In 1954, under law 12103, a separate district was created. Its capital was the town of Paratía and it incorporated the areas of Chanawayta, Koarita, Chawpiwayta, Chingani, Waraya, San Antonio, Alpakoyo, San José de Makalaka, Harpaña, Pakaje, Sora, and Hapo, taken from the districts of Lampa, Santa Lucía, and Pukará.

CHAPTER 2

MAN, CULTURE, AND SOCIETY

IN THIS CHAPTER we will briefly discuss the people and society of Paratía, sketching the cultural background of their lives as herders, weavers, and merchants.

The People of Paratía

We must make it clear at the outset that biometric studies were not conducted in Paratía, nor were others relating to physical anthropology. For this reason, we shall not plunge deeply into the interesting topic of man's biosomatic adaptation to an altitude of more than 4,300 meters.

Nonetheless, it is obvious that both men and women are quite strong and have tremendous stamina. They can easily travel up to forty kilometers a day, even while carrying heavy loads that surely exceed forty or fifty kilograms. They say it is more comfortable for them to walk over rugged, steep terrain than on flat surfaces, to climb up and down hills rather than walk on the pampas. And they seem to be right—when traveling with them, one sees the ease with which they climb hills, showing no great fatigue even when children are along. In level places, on the other hand, they reduce their pace. It might be worth mentioning that there are few cases of obesity, and even those who are fat tend not to be excessively overweight.

31

Parents and children comprise the basic social and residential unit in Paratía. Newlyweds usually live patrilocally for a few years, but eventually they build a separate homestead for themselves and their progeny. Although the birth rate is quite high, family size is limited by a high degree of infant mortality. The district's population, nonetheless, is relatively youthful and expanding. In fact, population growth may be a threat to the viability of the pastoral way of life in Paratía.

Demographic Characteristics

Existing data are incomplete, but those that follow will give an approximate idea of the population and its principal demographic characteristics. According to the Sixth National Population Census (CORPUNO 1964), Paratía has a total of 1,664 inhabitants, 769 men and 895 women. According to the same source, 187 people (110 men and 77 women) live in town and 1,477 people reside in the rural areas of the district (Table I).

Table I.   Population of Paratía

Population	Men	Women	Total
Urban Population	110	77	187
Rural Population	659	818	1,477
Total	769	895	1,664

To analyze the demographic situation we have used the statistical material collected during the smallpox vaccination campaign by the first aid officer, the *sanitario* of the Regional Health Agency stationed in Paratía, supplemented with data we obtained ourselves. The differences between these data and the figures from the official census are substantial but not critical, although in some cases—for example, the data referring to the town population—one can assume that the census was in error. Table II shows the population distribution by age according to our data.

The total population is 1,365 people: 623 men and 742 women. Women outnumber men by 119, and make up 54.36 percent of the population. There are more females born than males. This inequality continues throughout the years, except in the 40–50 age bracket, when males are slightly more numerous. After this period, the situation changes abruptly, and women are again predominant. It is interesting to note, in examining mortality figures, that the rate of female deaths is higher during the first 15 years and that of the males after 25 years, the age at which their numbers begin to decline rapidly, with very few men reaching old age.

Table II.   Age and Distribution of the Population of Paratía

Men	Age	Women	Total
103	0–4	132	235
101	5–9	115	216
91	10–14	89	180
41	15–19	71	112
52	20–24	65	117
28	25–29	43	71
35	30–34	52	87
41	35–39	40	81
45	40–44	37	82
34	45–49	25	59
9	50–54	17	26
12	55–59	12	24
12	60–64	16	28
4	65–69	13	17
9	70–74	6	15
1	75–79	2	3
3	80–84	2	5
—	85–89	1	1
1	90–94	2	3
—	95–99	—	—
—	100–104	2	2
1	?	—	1
623		742	1,365

If we take into account the fact that the childbearing capacity of women occurs between the ages of 15 and 45 years, in Paratía there are 308 women capable of reproducing. Hence, the birth rate is quite high. For example, in the period between January 1963 and July 1964, 119 children were born. In other words, 38.64 percent of the women capable of doing so reproduced. This results in quite a young population, as evidenced in the age column in Table II. The population below 15 years of age represents 46.23 percent of the total; those between 16 and 44 years of age represent 40.29 percent, even though they span a period of twice as many years; and finally, those 45 or older constitute only 13.48 percent of the population.

The youthfulness of the population creates various problems beyond the scope of our study. They are sufficiently important, however, to be outlined here. If the present rate of population growth continues, property, under the current system of inheritance, will be further and further subdivided. Since herds of alpaca need extensive lands for grazing, the reduction in the size of landholdings will result in fewer herds that can satisfy the basic needs of their owners.

The birth rate, as we have noted, is quite high. In 19 months, from January 1963 to July 1964, 119 children were born, 63 males and 56 females. Details on the timing of these births are found in Table III.

According to the Civil Registry of the District Municipality, 60 of the 119 births were to parents not married in accordance with the regulations of the current national Civil Code—an

Table III.   Births of Children by Month

Year	Month	Males	Females	Total
1963	January	6	4	10
	February	2	1	3
	March	3	4	7
	April	—	4	4
	May	6	3	9
	June	5	4	9
	July	6	5	11
	August	4	2	6
	September	5	—	5
	October	3	3	6
	November	5	3	8
	December	6	3	9
1964	January	2	4	6
	February	3	1	4
	March	2	1	3
	April	1	3	4
	May	1	3	4
	June	3	5	8
	July	—	3	3
		63	56	119

indication of the lack of influence official Peruvian marriage laws have on the indigenous culture, and the strength of the traditional customs.

Table IV.   Deaths by Month and Sex

Year	Month	Men	Women	Total
1963	January	3	—	3
	February	1	1	2
	March	2	2	4
	April	—	—	—
	May	1	3	4
	June	—	—	—
	July	—	2	2
	August	2	4	6
	September	—	1	1
	October	2	3	5
	November	2	2	4
	December	4	1	5
1964	January	5	3	8
	February	2	6	8
	March	5	3	8
	April	4	1	5
	May	1	2	3
	June	1	—	1
	July	1	—	1
		36	34	70

The mortality data in Table IV show a certain equality regarding the sexes of the deceased. Of the total, infants under one year of age, many only days or weeks old, constitute 43.82 percent. Those who died before the age of five make up more than half the total deaths during this period, 67.14 percent to be exact. Those under ten years, including those who died in their first year, account for a very high 71.42 percent. The aged, over fifty years old, represent only 21.42 percent. From these figures one can see that newborns have very little likelihood of reaching the age of five, although after this critical period they can hope to live without great danger to fifty, which appears to be the average lifespan.

The principal causes of death are pulmonary and respiratory illnesses, including violent attacks of hemoptysis, which is especially common among those over twenty-five. Infant mortality is frequently due to broncho-pulmonary diseases.

All these conclusions must be accepted with reservations, since our data come from the archives of the municipality. These records do not contain specialized medical information and do not require the presentation of death certificates, which would be impossible to obtain because there are no medical experts in the area. The diseases referred to above represent 68.75 percent of the causes of death and 74.46 percent of the deaths of those under five years of age. The remainder are produced by other diseases such as colic, diarrhea, and scarlet fever.

The annual birth rate is 63.7 per thousand, while the fertility rate reaches 76.26 per thousand. The mortality rate in general is 26.7 per thousand, while infant mortality reaches the high figure of 11.7 per thousand of total population.

In the period cited earlier, eighteen civil marriages were registered. By comparing the ages of the brides and grooms, one notes that there is a tendency for men to marry older women. Marital unions usually are endogamous at the district, hacienda, and hamlet levels.

In general, the population is quite mobile, because of the commercial ventures in which many Paratíans are involved. However, permanent emigration is still limited, although many youths, who have become aware of new possibilities through the schools, now leave in search of work, new opportunities, and adventure. The department of Arequipa, and especially its capital city, are the preferred destinations.

Because of this "migratory sifting," which follows sex lines, the majority of adult men have some familiarity with other places, principally from their commercial activities. Many, moreover, have visited the cities of Puno, Cuzco, Arequipa, and even Lima. On the other hand, women, following what appears to be a standard pattern for the department of Puno, have traveled little and do not know places farther from home than the provincial capital of Lampa, where they attend festivals, occasional commercial fairs, and religious celebrations. The mobility of the men has a fairly traditional character. Its primary objective is to supply the family with food.

According to the national census, Paratía has an "urban" population of 187 people, of which 77 are women and 110 are men. The results of our study reveal that the stable population of the capital does not exceed 52 people, 23 males and 29 females. But even this number fluctuates because there are school-age children and adults accompanying them who live in town only part of the time. These people leave when the school is closed—on weekends and during vacations in August and December—to return to their homes.

The town of Paratía has twenty blocks with a total of 110 houses. The 52 inhabitants are situated as follows:

1st Block	Uninhabited
2nd Block	Uninhabited
3rd Block	School complex
4th Block	3 males; 6 females
5th Block	Uninhabited
6th Block	3 males; 6 females
7th Block	Uninhabited
8th Block	Uninhabited
9th Block	Uninhabited
10th Block	3 males; 1 female
11th Block	1 male; 0 females
12th Block	4 males; 4 females
13th Block	Uninhabited
14th Block	6 males; 5 females
15th Block	Uninhabited
16th Block	Uninhabited
17th Block	2 males; 4 females
18th Block	1 male; 2 females
19th Block	Uninhabited
20th Block	Health post; 1 male

Of the total population, sixteen are children under five. These youngsters do not go to school; they are simply accompanying their mothers while the mothers live in town to care for children attending school. Of the remaining thirty-six inhabitants, approximately ten are adults. In the list of houses we have included residences which consist of only a single room. Ten families live more or less permanently in the town. The other inhabitants of the district live in dispersed compounds several kilometers apart. The two other places which can be considered as nucleated settlements are Koarita and Kilishani.

Quechua and Spanish

The language used in ordinary daily conversation is Quechua, or Runasimi. The local dialect has many constructions and sounds not found in Cuzco, perhaps because they have disappeared there or because of the influence of and borrowing from Aymara, the other native language of the Altiplano. Quechua is the language used within the home and with neighbors, friends, and fellow Paratíans. However, Spanish is preferred when dealing with mestizos and strangers and also in school. Nonetheless, the civil authorities and schoolteachers frequently must resort to Quechua in order to make sure they are completely understood.

Quechua-Spanish bilingualism is almost the exclusive prerogative of men, particularly those under fifty years of age. Most men between the ages of fifteen and forty-five speak Spanish. The women, as in many areas in the Peruvian highlands, generally cannot speak Spanish. Recently, some girls have begun to learn the "official" language of the country at school.

For the mestizos, Spanish is the mother tongue, but nonetheless they must often use Quechua words, phrases, and even whole sentences to express themselves clearly and precisely.

To illustrate the differences in the dialects, some words and phrases of the Quechua of Paratía are compared below to those of the Cuzqueño dialect. A list of all the differences could in itself be the subject of a separate study.

Paratía Quechua	Cuzco Quechua	Spanish	English
Uña pistantin	Wama marqasqa	Cargando a su criatura	Carrying his/her child
Pisititu	Pisicha	Poquito	Little
Pilluro	Piruro	Volanda de la rueca	Rapid twisting of the spindle
Kuñitan	Kunachallan	Ahorita	Right now
Warmisitunta	Warmachanta	A sus hijitos	To his/her little children
Yarvi	Wayri	Aguja grande	Large needle
K'upakuy	——	Pegar fuerte	To hit hard
K'ilo	——	Frío con cielo nublado	Cold with a cloudy sky
Lukli Kara	——	Ambicioso	Ambitious, greedy
Makisitunta	Maqichanta	Su manito	His/her little hand
Erkesitukuna	Erqequna	Los muchachos	The boys
Khari	Qosa	Esposo	Husband
Washkitallawan	Washkhallawan	Sólo con la soga	Only with the rope
Khewerkapuway	Marqapuway	Cárgamelo	Carry it for me
Khakaykuy	——	Encarcelar	To imprison
Lluylluska	——	Envuelto	Wrapped
Wallkushan	Warkushan	Colgando	Is hanging
K'anakushan	——	Cuando la alpaca levanta la cola	When the alpaca lifts its tail
Wachicito	Waraqa	Honda	Slingshot
Kuyay	——	Tener hijos de modo muy seguido	To have children in rapid succession

Charki and Chuño

In Paratía, the principal foods are those common throughout the Andean area, especially in southern Peru. The major part of the diet consists of plant foods acquired through trade, as well as some meat, but relatively little of the latter considering that the people of Paratía raise edible animals. The most important plant foods are potatoes (which become *chuño* when dehydrated), *kinuwa, oka, kañiwa,** wheat, barley, *isaño,* and corn.† Meat comes from alpacas, llamas, and sheep, and is eaten fresh as well as dried (similar to dried beef). Dried meat is called *chalona* when it is from sheep, or *charki* when it is from alpacas or llamas. Salt may or may not be used in the preparation of dried meat. The proper time for salting is during May and June, when the intense cold accelerates dehydration. The drying process can also be speeded up by subjecting the fresh meat to pressure, treading on it to extract the moisture more quickly. A relatively poor family may consume three or four alpacas a year. On the other hand, the well-to-do are accustomed to slaughtering up to one animal a month.

Paratíans use very little salt in preparing their food. A palate not accustomed to their diet would definitely notice the lack of salt, although it is occasionally used. Their food is seasoned only lightly with *ají* (chili pepper) or other spices. They do, however, use various kinds of edible clay dissolved in water to which they sometimes add salt. They like to serve this clay when eating baked potatoes. There are two kinds: one, called *chaqo* is rather grainy; the other, known as *phasalla,* is finer and tastier, and therefore preferred. The Paratíans drink infusions made from many wild plants such as *sallikata,* as well as tea and coffee. They eat small amounts of noodles, some rice, and occasionally bread acquired in the nearby towns or at the Sunday markets and periodic fairs.

Foodstuffs are kept in the storage room, which is usually

---

*In the Paratían dialect of Quechua *kañiwa* is the name of *Chenopodium cannihua, Chenopodium pallidicaule,* and *Chenopodium hastatum* (Pulgar 1946:114). In other areas, the word *kañagua* is used.

†*Kinuwa* (*Chenopodium quinoa*), written as *quinua* in Spanish and English, is a high-altitude grain indigenous to the Andes similar to the *kañiwa* discussed in the preceding footnote. *Oka* (*Oxalis crenata* and *Oxalis tuberosa*), also written as *oca,* is a native Andean tuber, as is *isaño* (*Tropaeolum tuberosum*). [Trans.]

next to the bedroom. Potatoes, *isaño*, *oka*, and *chuño* are stored in wool sacks, enough to last a year.

Meals are served three times a day. The major foods are cooked in the morning and the evening, and the morning meals are more substantial than the others. Preparations begin around five o'clock, when the hearth is lit to cook breakfast (*almuerzo*), which normally consists of several servings of soup. This may be accompanied by cups of *sallikata*, tea, or coffee, all of which are referred to as *unu qoñi* (hot water). The midday meal is light—sometimes leftovers from the morning's breakfast, but more often toasted and ground wheat or toasted beans and corn, boiled *chuño*, or *kañiwa*. In the afternoon, after five o'clock, there is another meal, which also consists of only one type of soup, with refillings of the bowl as desired.

The limited number of foodstuffs tends to restrict the variety of the local diet. The following are some examples of common dishes: the so-called "breakfast" (*almuerzo*) or *mikhuna*, which is boiled water with *papalisas,** *isaños*, and at times chunks of *chuño* added to give consistency to the broth; *chuño caldito*, a soup made almost exclusively of ground *chuño* with water, a little salt, and sometimes a piece of meat; *phiri*, made with a flour base, or *chilli-haku*, made of wheat or barley ground by themselves, mixed with alpaca blood, and roasted directly on top of the coals of the hearth or in kettles heated like an oven; and *toktochi*, made of flour and water, to which milk and eggs may be added to improve the quality and flavor—fried in oil, *toktochi* can be stored and is a highly prized food. The sausage called *yawal longani* is like black pudding; the intestines of the alpaca or llama are stuffed with a mixture of alpaca blood, flour, and salt. Unfortunately, this does not keep very well. *Patas-kaldu* is a soup made by boiling the feet and lower legs of an alpaca in water with toasted corn. *Kankachu*, or "roast," prepared usually with quarters of alpaca, llama, or sheep, using little or no condiments, is roasted directly over the coals and is a delicacy. *K'ispiño* is made from ground *kañiwa*, water, lime,

---

Papalisa (*Ullucus tuberosus*), sometimes called *ulluco* or *lisas*, is a tuber raised at high altitudes. [Trans.]

and salt—these ingredients are molded by hand into small cakes which can be kept for a long time. Together with *toktochi*, *k'ispiño* forms the basic provision on extended trading trips. At times, *k'ispiño* is kneaded with milk and cooked in steam. *Phuti* is a boiled food made of *oka*, *isaño*, and *kinuwa*. When alpacas, llamas, or sheep are castrated, their testicles are boiled and eaten. *Tostado* is toasted wheat or barley; it can be ground on a flat stone called a *khona*, which is laid across the knees and used with another smaller flat stone called a *luriya* which functions as a mano, very much like the metate used by women in Central America. The flour produced in this way is sometimes passed through a sieve or sifter and kept to be eaten at midday or during trips.

Some foods are recommended for certain conditions. For example, *kinuwa* broth is suggested for nursing mothers since it is said to increase their milk. The same property is attributed to *chuño* and rice broth. Trout, a relatively new addition to the diet, is recommended for convalescences and cases of relapse in illnesses or in the recovery from childbirth. Women who have recently given birth are urged not to use salt in their food. Finally, Paratíans greatly enjoy candy and chewing gum.

Water for domestic use comes from springs near the houses or from streams and rivers. Since clothes are washed and excrement dumped in the same streams, the drinking water is often contaminated.

Adult men and women drink a good deal of alcohol. The former, especially at religious fiestas and family gatherings, down great quantities of *waqto*, a mixture of alcohol and water. Other drinks, such as anise brandy, rum, and cognac, are also popular. To demonstrate esteem for visitors and friends (and as a form of conspicuous consumption), Paratíans serve beer. Whey they go on a trip, most men carry small bottles (*cuartos*) of cognac or alcohol, which they frequently put to use. The large consumption of alcohol is not limited to the natives; the mestizos also drink a lot, and it is difficult to state precisely who drinks the most. Perhaps the mestizos do, since the Indians tend to restrict their drinking to religious fiestas, family re-unions, and occasional visits to nearby towns or to Paratía itself.

The mestizos do not need these pretexts—for them any occasion is suitable.

Paratíans often chew coca leaves. The women seem to chew more than the men, particularly when they are weaving, undoubtedly to alleviate their weariness from this exhausting task. The men chew more coca when they drink or are involved in activities requiring strength, e.g., the manufacture of adobes, the construction of houses, the installation of roofs, or the shearing of alpacas. The act of chewing coca is called *akully*. To give it a special flavor and to make it sweet they add *llipta*,* acquired in towns and at fairs.

Cigarettes, especially the cheap brands, are common, but smoking tobacco does not seem to be habitual for these people. Instead, they smoke at special events, and a cigarette is always considered a good gift. Both men and women smoke.

Coca and tobacco have other uses as medicines and as part of the paraphernalia used during magical or religious ceremonies. In medicines they are utilized as matés, in rubbing, and in poultices. In divination, coca is the key element used to predict the future or to explain the past; it is for this reason that such practices are called "examining the coca."

Trout and Vicuñas

The natives of Paratía do not hunt because, as will be seen later, their magico-religious beliefs prevent them from killing wild animals. The mestizos, including the local authorities, the ranchers, the teachers, and perhaps a few well-acculturated natives, do hunt. Many of them, hunting illegally, have exterminated entire herds of vicuñas. *Vizcachas* and deer are hunted for diversion and for their delicious meat; pumas, however, are feared by all. It is not unusual for the natives to ask mestizos to

---

*A catalyst to release the active substances in coca, *llipta* is chewed in small amounts with each bolus of coca leaves. *Llipta* is generally made from the burnt stalks of the *kinuwa* plant. The ashes are mixed with water; this concoction then hardens into rocklike blocks. [Trans.]

exterminate the *vizcachas* and in this way prevent them from consuming pastures reserved for the alpacas.

In the rivers trout fishing is intense, even during the season when it it prohibited. Originally trout were eaten only by mestizos and those natives familiar with this type of food. Today fish is slowly becoming accepted, above all because trout is considered *misti* (mestizo) food and to eat it confers a certain prestige.

Children and youths devote much time and interest to fishing, but most adults do not consider it a serious endeavor. Many fishing techniques are used, including illegal explosives and the little known method of striking the water with a cudgel. Dynamite is used only by mestizos and very few natives. Some fishermen, through outside contacts, have learned to use nets, which are stretched across the river from bank to bank, trapping great quantities of fish in a short time. This technique is not widespread and appears to be a recent introduction. Most of the people use sharp, pointed hooks made of iron, tied to thick string. These are submerged in deep places or pools in the rivers and pulled sharply to pierce the fish—they are not fishhooks because they are too large. The natives scare the fish by throwing stones, directing the fish to the spot where the hook awaits them. Another technique, used mostly by children, is to catch fish with one's bare hands. To be successful, one must be able to withstand the cold water and have the help of some friends. But the most unusual technique—used by some children, youths, and, at times, adults—consists of hitting the water with big clubs. The frightened fish are caught with the same sticks, are pressed against the rocks in the river, or are killed outright by the concussion produced by the sticks beating on the water.

Cabins, Homesteads, and Town

Herding requires regular changes of pasture, driving the herds to the best grass. Since the care of the animals calls for constant vigilance, the herder must remain very near his herds of alpacas and llamas; as they move in search of grass, the herder, too, must be on the move. For this reason the people have various homes, when possible one in each of their herding areas (*ahijaderos*). But this does not mean that all their activities and belongings need to move along with the herds. Instead, there will be one main house, known as the *estancia* (homestead). The seasonal huts in the herding sectors, called *cabañas* (cabins), are secondary homes. In addition, each family usually maintains a house in the town of Paratía.

The *cabañas* are isolated and only occupied occasionally. Built beside the corrals in the herding area, they are rustic structures with stone walls made with mud mortar, and roofs of straw resting on frames of *kewña* (*Popylepis* sp.) poles. They are usually about twelve to fourteen square meters; the floors of the rooms are lower than ground level by about twenty-five centimeters and at times more. The doors are very low, so that it is necessary to bend quite a bit to enter a house. Sometimes additional rooms on the side are used as the kitchen or living quarters by other members of the family who take care of the animals. When the huts are to be used, the roofs must be repaired and doors and other fixtures replaced, since nothing is left behind at the *cabañas* when they are not in use. Everything is carried in—cooking utensils, provisions, fuel, quilts, and much more.

The homestead is the permanent residence, where the family dwells and where most of its possessions are kept. In building a home compound, Paratíans look for "low" places near springs or streams, and in the vicinity of their kinsmen's homesteads. They prefer to be within sight of a neighbor's house. Depending on the configuration of the land, it may be possible to see homesteads many kilometers in the distance. When a number of homesteads have been built somewhat close together, a school is established; and in accordance with the administrative systems of the Peruvian government, these settlements have begun to be called *anexos, caserios,* or *parcialidades*.

The homesteads are groups of rooms built around a main patio; the spaces between the rooms serve as entryways. One of the spaces is always distinguished as the central entrance. The

Paratíans have temporary residences in herding areas distant from their permanent homes. These *cabañas* are rather crude structures, built of uncut stone and covered with a straw roof. At the beginning of the season they must first be repaired, the thatch must be renewed, the door must be replaced, and supplies and equipment must be hauled from the permanent residence.

The main homestead for the Paratían family, known as the *estancia,* generally consists of several independent one-room buildings grouped around an open patio. These buildings are surrounded by extensive corrals. Techniques used in constructing *estancia* huts and *cabañas* are similar, but the former tend to be larger and better outfitted. The number of rooms and the complexity of the corrals are also greater in the *estancias.*

houses are surrounded by corrals, and there are small lean-to structures serving as a refuge for dogs as well as chickens. The walls are of rough, uncut stones held together by either mud mortar or adobes. The floors of the rooms are below ground level. The doors may be made of boards taken from crates, thin wooden rods tied together with leather straps or nailed, or, rarely, sheets of corrugated zinc (*calamina*). Many doors seem merely symbolic—they do not offer much protection against intruders. If the owner is well-to-do, he may buy doors of wood planks in the town of Santa Lucía or in Juliaca. The roof always has a frame of *kewña* poles, brought from Palca or some other neighboring area. These are tied one against another with leather strips or straw ropes, forming something like "rooster feet." On gabled roofs, the poles form a very rustic crosswork. The framework of the roof is covered with straw, which is also brought from outside the area because the local straw is very short and not very fit for roofing. Roofing in itself is work reserved for the men, and although the women may help, they are not permitted to climb on top of the houses because it could bring bad luck. After arranging the bundles of straw in place, the natives secure them by means of thick straw ropes daubed with mud and woven from one side to the other, passing over the ridge pole. The ropes are known as *kawallo* (horse) or *wasi hapina* (house graspers). Roofing is done in a single day, and usually lasts no more than ten hours for an ordinary one-room house. It is an occasion to organize fiestas with much food, drink, and music. Roofs generally are good for three or four years, with yearly repairs; after this time, they must be rebuilt. This is known as *t'ikraska*. After finishing a roof, the Paratíans carry out ceremonies to appease the spirits; it is a happy time, with music, dancing, drinking, and eating. For this work people enlist their relatives, neighbors, and friends in *minka*, a form of reciprocal exchange.

The size of the rooms is variable: some are two or three meters on a side, others five or six meters by three meters; the average height of the walls is no more than 180 centimeters, without taking into account the angle of the roof.

The hearth is on the floor or at times on a platform. The

only exits for smoke are the door and a little opening in one of the walls or the roof which at the same time serves as a source of light. Whenever possible, openings in the roof or walls are avoided to prevent the cold wind from entering. The floor, at a lower level than the ground outside, is made of packed earth; on it are scattered many of the household goods and utensils such as clay pots and dishes, perhaps one or two metal dishes, many bottles, alcohol cans, and sacks. On top of the sleeping platform (*phata khawa*) are bedclothes: homemade blankets and an item called the *thanako,* or *Arequipa palio,* made from a mass of old clothing sewn together. While it is occasionally possible to find a metal or wooden bed, it is rare to see anyone sleep on it—Paratíans prefer to sleep on the floor or on an adobe platform. They are accustomed to sleeping with their faces wrapped up, although their feet may be left uncovered.

From the walls and the roof hang a large assortment of baskets, bundles containing small domestic goods, skeins of wool, fleeces, garments, and a hundred other things. Niches in the walls serve as closets. Wooden furniture is scarce, but sometimes there is a small table. In one of the corners of the room dry dung and bits of kindling wood are stacked almost to the ceiling. Small domestic animals, sometimes guinea pigs or chickens and always dogs, scamper about the floor, sharing the same roof with their masters. In a few instances one finds a sewing machine, more often a transistor radio, and, rarely, a typewriter or camera. The huts and rooms of the homesteads generally take on the aroma of the stored hides and fleeces.

Houses in the town of Paratía differ only slightly from those described above. Almost all are of adobe, with straw roofs mounted like those of the rural homesteads. The rooms are erected around a central patio, although on a more regular plan. Sometimes the doors have been painted. The windows may contain metal frames and glass. The houses' dimensions are similar to those of the homesteads; their small doors, windows, and access steps make them seem like doll houses. Five of these houses have roofs made of corrugated zinc sheets, symbols of prestige which announce the economic status of the proprietors.

There are no more than four houses with two stories, and some of these are not finished due to the scarcity of wood for the floors. The outside walls of the houses are painted with colored earth dissolved in water. However, this paint washes off with the first rains. For the national holiday in July, the municipal authorities insist that the walls of all the houses be painted. Frequently they are decorated with pictures of the national flag, allegories with human figures, or representations of animals, plants, and houses. The kitchens tend to be somewhat smaller than the other rooms and are dedicated exclusively to cooking. Attached to other buildings one often finds doghouses and chicken pens. The corrals for the herds are made of stone like those on the homesteads.

Most families have houses of this sort, which they occupy when they need to be in town for a period of time or simply when they spend a night there during a fiesta or other special occasion. However, the houses receive such infrequent use that the walls are falling into ruin and the roofs are caving in, giving Paratía the look of a ghost town. Another sign of infrequent habitation is that the padlocks on the doors are sealed with clay for security.

The construction of dwellings is accompanied by magical ceremonies to appease the spirits so they will protect the inhabitants. Upon laying the first stone of the foundation, the natives offer *tinka** to the *apu* (gods). When the building is finished, they pass the night keeping watch and pouring libations while listening to the music of mandolins and the *kirkincho* (a small instrument of wood and strings, called a *charango* in Spanish), in this way hoping to frighten off any demons. As a sign of dedication and protection, a cross attached to the tie-beam is hung with offerings—small bottles of alcohol; miniature woolen sacks with potatoes, *chuño,* and corn meal (*maná*); and paper decorations.

Tinka is a ritual act in which an offering is made by pouring a few drops of alcohol, usually 89 percent ethyl alcohol or wine, on the ground or on the object to be blessed. [Trans.]

Skirt and Red Poncho

The natives like to wear colorful costumes at festival times. They boast that their dress is the most elegant in the whole department of Puno, and we would not disagree. Some of these garments, with their marvelous combinations of colors and great variety of ornaments, are truly works of art. In spite of the fact that black and blue are the most common colors, the overall pattern of the cloth, with its designs and decorations, shows such a range of hues that it is almost as if a rainbow had been snatched and woven into the cloth.

From the moment the natives are old enough to notice it, the quality and cost of clothing become important in several ways. High quality clothing confers prestige on the wearer and shows his economic status. Clothing is a form of conspicuous consumption in which Paratíans invest long hours of work and valuable materials. Not everyone can afford these refinements; many resign themselves to simpler garments, or in the worst cases to doing without some of them.

There are two main types of clothing, for daily or ordinary use and for festivals. This is true for both men and women, although the difference is less generally visible among the men because of the great similarity between everyday suits and those worn for festivals.

Clothes can also be classified according to the age and sex of the wearer. However, clothing is rather similar for boys and girls, especially at an early age, since it is made from old adult clothing cut into swaddling clothes, with the addition of a knitted wool cap. During infancy both sexes wear the *wara* or *phalika,* a rectangular cloth wrapped around the body and fastened in the middle by a woven belt (*chumpi*). The color reserved for boys is white, while red is for girls. This is a rather widespread custom, and it is possible to determine the sex of children by the color of their *wara.* The *phalika* are used until the age of five or six, when boys begin to wear homespun pants and girls graduate to woven skirts, *aqsu,* of black or brown wool with multicolored bands at the hem and waist. The mothers expend a great deal of effort on these garments, weaving them with twelve to fifteen lines of magnificently blended colors. The method involved in this is unique: they are woven in two equal pieces that are later joined in the middle by nearly invisible seams. It is interesting to note, by the way, that the Incan name given to these skirts was *aqsu*, a name which is still used in Paratía. Some drawings by Guamán Poma de Ayala (1956:355, 359–360, and 363) show women's skirts with parallel lines in the hem identical to those we have described.

After they are about five years old, boys begin to wear shirts of homespun (*bayeta*), either pure white or with decorative designs worked in combinations of natural-colored wool. They also wear hats of sheep wool or felt. Underclothes are uncommon, save for one type of long-legged trousers worn under the pants. At night or on cold days, men wear small ponchos made of undyed alpaca wool. On their feet are sandals of untanned alpaca or llama leather, cut from one piece, with the wool on the outside, and tied at the ankles with strings. The *chaqe*, as they are called, generally are cut from the neck of the hide because it is stronger and more durable. The hide is moistened, the *chaqe* are cut, and they are worn immediately. After drying they retain the shape of the wearer's feet. This type of footgear provides little protection; the feet are not covered sufficiently to ward off the cold, and when it rains or snows the sandals get wet quickly, causing more bother than comfort. Sandals are worn by children and adults, men as well as women, although youths now prefer footwear made of tanned hide. Guamán Poma de Ayala (1956:477–478) also documented the *chaqe*, especially at the festival of the Qollasuyos and Condesuyos, where his drawings show men and women using them for dancing.

In addition to their skirts (*aqsu*), girls wear homespun blouses dyed red and black, called *jubonilla*. On top of these, on cold days or at night, they wrap woven shawls pinned at the chest with large brooches, sometimes of silver. Their hats are made of felt and cloth and are bought in the nearby towns or at fairs.

The transition of youths to adult status is signaled by fundamental changes in dress. The transition occurs around the age of fifteen or sixteen for girls, when they start to use a *montera* in place of a felt hat.* The cloth hats, as the name suggests, are undoubtedly of Spanish origin; their profusion of adornments and multicolored decorations makes them highly attractive. The frame, made of straw and cloth, is obtained from the hatmakers of Calapuja, a town near Juliaca, and at fairs. The women of Paratía later adorn them themselves, sewing the front and back parts with two *t'ika* (flowers) made of strands of *colones* (colored ribbons) and dyed alpaca wool. Along the sides they sew very artistic embroideries, called *mat'e*, made of colored beads or "pearls," and crossed by multicolored threads. On the brims are more small beads, forming intricate designs which add to the beauty of the whole. Hats worn every day differ from those for fiestas mainly in the quantity, quality, and variety of decorations. When not in use, fiesta hats are stored carefully in cloth or plastic cases to protect them. It is not uncommon to see a woman wearing a hat still wrapped in its protective covering or wearing her everyday hat and carrying a new one in her hands, reserved for the moment of the fiesta. When a woman has used a hat long enough, she takes off the decorations and they become part of a new hat.

The adult woman's *jubonilla* (from the Spanish *jubón,* jacket) is a dark blue and black jacket lavishly adorned with embroidered threads and colored buttons. The decoration is in rows and geometric figures, and the golden metal buttons add to the garment's striking appearance. The metal buttons are rare because they are not available commercially, and their price is very high, up to ten soles each (in 1964). If one takes into consideration the fact that a rather modest *jubonilla* has on the average more than 250 buttons, one will clearly understand the high economic value such a garment acquires, even if the worth of only some of the materials is calculated, without assessing the value of the time spent acquiring the materials and making the garment.

---

*Altiplano *monteras* usually have a low crown and a broad brim. They are made of woven wool and/or cotton. The felt hats referred to in this passage have high crowns and narrow brims. [Trans.]

Paratían men and women wear their most highly decorated clothes when attending fiestas. The ponchos men use on such occasions are covered with intricate designs, both geometric and naturalistic. Although these garments are multicolored, red predominates. The men's pants are made of dark homespun and adorned with buttons along slits made between the cuff and the knee. Women wear the *jubonilla*, a short jacket in blue or black that is heavily decorated with rows of colorful buttons and embroidered designs. Over the *jubonilla* they wear a *llijlla*, a woven shawl that displays their artistic abilities to the fullest. Their fiesta skirts, *polleras*, have multicolored bands around the hem and at the waist. For a woman's outfit to be complete, she must have a *montera*, a hat that is richly ornamented. Both men and women may wear one or more *ch'uspa*, a bag in which coca leaves are carried.

Under the *jubonilla,* blouses of ordinary cloth are worn; these are usually made of homespun. Over the *jubonilla,* hanging from the head, is the *chuko,* falling from under the hat almost to the ankles. The *chuko* is a rectangular cloth made of homespun and decorated with colored threads called *batanés,* or *chuko t'ika,* which hang from the edges. The *llijlla* (shawl) is slung on top of the *jubonilla* and *chuko.* This is a skillfully woven garment which displays the women's many talents—the variety of decorative motifs and colors is enormous. *Llijllas* are made in two equal halves which are later sewn together, leaving sections at the ends that are incompletely woven because of the techniques used in weaving. When the sun is bright and hot, the women use small woven shawls they call *phullu* as a means of protection. These are draped over the top of the hat.

The *llijlla* is fastened at the chest by means of a big *tupu* (silver brooch), or at times a pin. The skirts (*polleras*) are of the same colors as the *chuko* and the *jubonilla,* with multicolored bands sewn on the hem as on the *aqsu* skirts. This last technique is fairly recent, begun not more than twenty years ago. The skirt is fastened at the waist with cords sewn into the skirt itself. Underneath, the women wear more skirts, in many cases up to ten. These are simpler; those for daily use have no more than a fringe sewn on the border. As with the *llijlla,* the skirts are generally worn with the face towards the inside, that is to say, inside out. This prevents the sun from bleaching them out, since the chemicals used in dyeing the wool are not very durable and fade easily.

The difference between fiesta clothing and ordinary clothing is in the quantity of decorations. Basically the materials are identical; the cut is the same; moreover, it is customary for a fiesta outfit that has been used heavily to become an everyday garment. When a close kinsman dies, one form of showing grief is to wear hats without any decoration and skirts of only one color, or turned inside out.

When men are considered adult they can wear fiesta clothes. Their hats are particularly interesting; they are now very hard to buy because there are no craftsmen who can make them. Hence, hats are zealously kept and cared for and worn with great vanity. The hat's crown is high, the top is wider than the bottom, and the brim is flat. Hats are also covered with *colones,* or braided bands, in a variety of geometric patterns. From the brims hang tassels identical to those on the women's hats. The crown is surrounded by a wide band with embroidery made of metallic pieces and colored threads, called *toquillo,* which probably corresponds to the Spanish *toquilla,* or gauze. Under the hat is the *chullu,* or cap, without earflaps, which usually is white with red designs. The *chullu* comes to a sharp point, from which many ribbons hang.

The men wear short jackets that reach to the tops of their belts; called *chamarra* (possibly from the Spanish *zamarra,* a sheepskin jacket), they are made of black or dark blue homespun and are adorned with fillets on the sleeves, embroidery, and metal buttons—easily as many as 150 or 200 identical to those used on the women's *jubonilla.* The pants, of the same material as the *chamarra,* have slits along the legs starting at the calf, hence their name, *khalla pantalon* (cut-off pants); such trousers are described for the *chiris* of Ichu (Cuentas 1956:135), and the style appears to have been widespread in the department of Puno. The openings in the legs of the trousers are rimmed with embroidery, fillets, and more than a hundred metal buttons. Underneath, men wear white homespun underwear which helps to keep the slits open, giving the illusion that they are wearing chaps. The pants are fastened at the waist with a *chumpi,* a woven woolen belt with colored designs.

On top of the *chamarra* the men wear beautiful red ponchos with wonderfully intricate figures and color combinations. They are woven more for show than for protection. Usually Paratíans wear them on fiesta days, but they are also worn inside out when it is very sunny. On top of the poncho and around the neck a triangular white cloth, called *pañuelo* (handkerchief), is tied. This provides protection from the sun.

When *ayarachi* groups are formed, the members dress in standard fiesta clothes, making some small alterations which we will discuss later.

Both men and women carry multicolored bags (*ch'uspa*) woven of wool, profusely decorated, and fringed with huge numbers of threads. These bags contain coca leaves. The women carry them in their hands, and the men have them hanging across their chests or from their necks. Without a *ch'uspa* an outfit would be incomplete, and a person would not appear in public. Both men's and women's clothes are made by part-time (never full-time) specialists, although ideally a woman should be able to sew and weave her own clothing. Men's clothing is sewn by certain specialists, and the red ponchos are woven by a man's mother, sister, or wife.

On ordinary days men wear pants and jackets made of homespun in black, white, or a black-and-white combination. The ponchos are woolen and known as *misti poncho*. Sheep's wool ponchos are preferred because they are said to shed the rain better and to be almost impermeable, a quality slightly less true of those woven with alpaca wool, which, on the other hand, are warmer. The men frequently wear factory-made underwear and the women undershirts of cotton or homespun.

The local fiesta clothes, particularly the men's, bear a certain resemblance to some European clothing, particularly that worn by Iberian men of an earlier period. This is probably due to the influence of Europeans who mined in the area and also to the decrees of the colonial government following the revolution of Túpac Amaru:

There was no great variation in the indigenous clothing until 1780: for men, the tunic (*unku*) and the cloak (*llakolla*) were the essential components of dress, as was the shawl (*llijlla*) among the women; but with the suppression of the great revolution led by the Indo-Peruvian Túpac Amaru, many drastic measures were taken to "de-Indianize" the population. Among these was the prohibition of native dress, which was replaced by the Spanish coat, pants, and hat for the men, and skirts and short jackets for the women, who were able to retain their primitive *llijlla*. [Valcárcel 1964a:172]

It would seem, therefore, that the present style of dress is a carry-over of the Iberian dress of earlier centuries. It represents the survival of a pattern from other times to which the natives have nevertheless given their own characteristic touch.

Birth and Death

As in all cultures and societies, man's passage through the various stages of life is surrounded with cultural events created by the group of people in which he lives and into which he entered by virtue of his birth.

Contraceptives are not used in Paratía. Although people have the idea that the use of ether can cause abortions, births are hardly ever prevented. Male children are preferred; this is explained by saying that "it is better," or that women "suffer" because often they will have children when they are still young or that, on the other hand, they sometimes cannot find husbands.

The moment of birth is a very private affair for the expectant mother. At times she will be assisted by her mother, perhaps by her husband, or, upon rare occasions, by another member of the family or a healer (*curandero*). After the labor pains begin, the woman remains at home, lying on bedclothes that have been spread out on the floor. If the birth is impeded by the position of the fetus or other complications, a specialist uses massage and manipulation to get the fetus into a suitable position. If, in spite of this effort, the birth still does not take place, magical ceremonies to facilitate delivery are performed. However, it is claimed that births are generally relatively quick and without complications. The newborn is received by the attendant and is placed on the blankets where the mother is lying.

The umbilical cord is cut with a knife, or sometimes scissors, to which strands of red wool have been tied for magical purposes. If the baby does not cry, it is rubbed first on the forehead and then on the mouth with Florida water (*agua florida*). Because of certain magical beliefs, Paratíans do not prepare a wardrobe of any kind before the birth, and the child is wrapped in rags from the used clothing of the older members of the family. Later, small covers and shirts are bought or knitted, but the swaddling clothes are made from used homespun woolens and remnants.

When the placenta has been expelled, it is washed with hot

water and later buried in a hole dug at the side of the door, along with the blood and urine from the first four days after delivery. If these precautions are not taken, the newly delivered woman could suffer from an infection of the genital organs, and the health of her child might be endangered. For the same reason, she should avoid seeing light and breathing fresh air because both she and the child could become ill. To lessen the pain and ensure that "everything inside closes up," the mother's head is wrapped with a scarf, cloth, or *llijlla*.

After a few days a specialist is summoned. Using *kollpa* (a white mineral), he rubs the mother's body from head to toe. It is said that this procedure guarantees that all internal ailments will leave her body. At the time of the massage, spirits are invoked so that sickness will not return. After finishing the operation, the specialist leaves the house and does not return for a certain period of time. If he were to come back before the time was over, he would bring the sickness with him.

For the child's protection, the house, the mother, and her baby undergo a ritual, the *tinka*. Next, everyone present is perfumed with incense and special herbs. The child is named after the Catholic saint on whose day he was born; the name is determined by consulting a calendar with saints' days. From then on the child is called by his own name, although a diminutive form or nickname is generally used. The birth is entered in the Civil Registry as soon as possible.

The mother gets up from her bed after fifteen days, but she is not allowed outside until a month has passed. If she does not take care of herself she could suffer a relapse and even lose her life; this means that she should not exercise very much, must avoid the cold and the wind, and take many other precautions for her health. Her food should contain little salt; she should eat lots of broth and *kinuwa* (in the form of *pesque*, a porridge), and above all *chuño* with rice, to ensure that she has plenty of milk to nurse the newborn child. In the first few days, the baby is fed with sugar water soaked into a dampened cloth. For sleeping, the infants are wrapped with their hands and feet tightly bound against the body.

When the mother gets up and leaves the sickbed for good,

she resumes her normal activity without any great change. The child receives her attention when it cries, since crying is interpreted as a sign of hunger, and the baby should be fed whenever it is hungry. The mother does not abandon her work to nurse the child, but tries instead to continue working at the same time. She will also nurse the infant in order to keep it quiet and prevent it from causing trouble. Variety is introduced into the child's diet at about six months, when it is given a little *kinuwa* broth boiled with a touch of salt. Before the infant is a year old it is sucking pieces of meat and eating many of the same foods as adults. When it defecates, the baby is cleaned with its own diaper, which is then doubled over and reused on the other side. Baths are rare and when they occur the child is immersed in a basin of warm water and washed with a dampened cloth.

Catholic baptism, or *unuchakuy*, is performed during the religious fiestas. The godparents tend to be natives, although at times mestizos are asked. This ritual creates kin-like relationships with strong rights and obligations among the godparents and godchildren and their respective family groups.

Children are not pressured to learn to walk; they crawl over the floor and stand on their own without any special encouragement from their elders. But when they fall and begin to cry, they are quickly attended to. If the outburst is severe, they are pacified by breastfeeding.

Wherever she goes, the mother will carry her child on her back, placing it on the ground when she has work to do. Weaning varies with the desires of the mother; sometimes breastfeeding continues until the child is two or three years old. When the child is to be weaned, the mother's nipples are coated with bitter or hot substances.

At the age of five or six, children stop wearing the *phalika* and put on skirts and pants, depending on their sex, and begin to be treated in accordance with their new status in society. Both male and female children start to help with tasks in the home, doing small domestic chores such as peeling potatoes, bringing water for cooking, lighting the fire, washing dishes, collecting wood and manure, and taking care of younger brothers and sisters. Boys are initiated into herding at the age of five or six, and before they reach ten are taking part in trading trips.

The haircutting ceremony, *chujcharutuchi,* takes place before the seventh birthday and sometimes coincides with the exchange of the *phalika* for skirt or pants. The godfather of the first haircutting gives alpacas to his godchild; these will form part of the godchild's future herd. If any of the animals die, it is the responsibility of the father to replace them. In this way, the child has animals which will multiply through the years and develop into a herd large enough so that he can support a wife and raise children. The *chujcharutuchi,* in which spiritual kinship bonds and friendship ties are established and strengthened, is always an opportunity for celebration.

Children are not physically punished with spankings; instead, obedience and discipline are demanded by raising one's voice. Grandchildren maintain an easy camaraderie with their grandparents, who may be extremely permissive and indulgent. When children become angry, they cry and shout, throw things on the floor, and hurl insults as their elders do. Children are able to care for themselves quite early in life. This can be seen very clearly among those who go to school—groups of related youngsters may live together and carry out the necessary chores, such as preparing meals and settling arguments, and in general take on adult responsibilities. This leads to a greater sense of maturity and self-sufficiency.

There is a good deal of interaction between children and adults. Groups consisting solely of children are rare, except when they are attending school. Because of this, children reach social maturity at a very early age. Nothing related to normal daily life is unknown to them; learning about sex, conception, and birth is no problem. Their sexual experiences begin early—boys generally start with an older woman—and are treated openly and without deception. The girls' first experiences are usually with older men.

The transition from childhood to adulthood is marked by several important steps. When a boy reaches the age of seventeen or eighteen, he is allowed to wear the red poncho (*poncho colorado*) and the fiesta dress as a symbol of his coming of age. He can then begin to pasture his own herd of alpacas and is ready to seek a wife. In the same way, when girls reach maturity at fifteen or sixteen they can wear fiesta clothing and enter into marriage. When old age and its accompanying disintegration of physical and mental faculties set in, a person is not abandoned by his family. The maintenance and care of the aged fall to the children, who provide for them and treat them with respect and consideration. Older people are allowed to do as they please. In exchange, they help with small jobs, such as collecting dung, spinning, and taking care of the kitchen, the house, and the children. It is common to see older people and children walking together, both engaged in the same kind of work.

When a person dies, the body is washed and placed on the floor of the house on a poncho, surrounded with candles. At the wake, the mourners make a great deal of noise in order to scare away evil spirits and to prevent further deaths. Bottles of drinks are placed as offerings at the feet and head of the corpse so that God may receive the soul. Before anyone drinks from the bottles, the body undergoes a *tinka;* drops of liquid are sprinkled at the sides and over the feet and head of the corpse. The first bottle is then tendered by the widow if the deceased is a man, by the parents if it is a child, and by the husband if it is a woman. The corpse is made to "drink" from a cup, and later all those present at the wake will also drink from it. Those who attend the wake bring bottles of alcohol or other drinks, which are matched by similar drinks at the expense of the family. Incense is burned in a small clay plate, and the smoke is believed to cleanse the body. Finally, the corpse is wrapped in a shroud, white homespun wool if unmarried or a child and blue if adult or married. During the wake, the guests talk about the deceased and his life. They are sad if the departed died without leaving any final instructions, for then no last wishes can be carried out.

In order to prevent the smell of the corpse from becoming unpleasant, its head is wrapped in a damp alpaca hide tied around the neck. The hands are placed on the chest, and the body is wrapped in ponchos or blankets and tied with ropes. If the deceased was wealthy, a coffin is made from old crates or is bought in one of the nearby towns. The friends and relatives are in charge of digging the grave. The burial is called *chinka-ripuchinku* (the disappearance). There is no set rule as to the length of time between death and burial. Before the funeral procession leaves for the cemetery, each relative purifies the corpse with incense which has been burned in a clay bowl (*chuwa*).

To carry the body to its final resting place, the male relatives dress in dark blue or black clothes, with ponchos to match. The women wear modest *jubonillas,* and their skirts are worn inside out so that only the blue or black side can be seen. Also, a black *llijlla* and a hat with no decorative bands will be worn by women at the funeral and by the widow for the next three months. The funeral procession is followed by a large number of children and curiosity-seekers. Friends and relatives carry bottles of alcohol and soft drinks, crackers, and candy. After an improvised prayer or without any religious ceremony, the body is deposited in the grave. A *llijlla* containing many small bags of *chuño,* flour, salt, *kinuwa,* barley, meat, and eggs, and bottles of alcohol is placed under the corpse's head like a pillow, so that the deceased "will have the means with which to journey through the other life." Then all the beverages are passed out among those present; sweets and soft drinks are given to the children as a show of gratitude for having accompanied the deceased to the cemetery. When the time comes to cover the grave, everyone present throws fistfuls of dirt on the body "so that one day someone will cover us too." Only dirt is thrown; the stones removed during the digging are left aside. If at the end there is not enough dirt to fill the grave, it is considered an evil omen. This terrifies the people because it means that the earth needs more dead. But when the grave can be filled with dirt, all is calm.

After the burial, the mourners remain in the cemetery drinking and talking with a great deal of noise and even some laughter. None of the participants is permitted to leave until every bottle has been emptied. The drinks must not be poured on the ground—everything must be drunk. Before the mourners return to the house, the tomb is cleaned very carefully and all footprints are wiped away, since the relatives will return at midnight to check for any new marks. If there are human prints it means that there will be another death soon in the family. If animal prints are seen, the departed will carry off all his animals. In either case, the family is filled with fear.

Upon returning to the house after the burial, the mourners pass by a running stream where they wash their feet, hands, and face. This keeps death at a distance and prevents it from catching up with them. The water purifies and protects them. After bathing, the relatives—male and female—change their clothes to remove themselves even further from death. For all intents and purposes, the somber part of the funeral ends here, and a different mood takes over. The people begin to talk more cheerfully, declaring that there is no reason to be sad since the death was caused by divine will. When they arrive at the house, blessings are exchanged in a ritual called *parabien*. People talk about the deceased without displaying pain or sadness. Instead there are smiles, jokes, laughter, and always drinking, since "it is for the best" and "there is no reason to be sorrowful."

On the eighth day there is usually a ceremony in the afternoon, which varies in its ostentation depending on the wealth and status of the deceased. The house is swept, preferably at the hour of the death. This is to keep death at a distance once and for all and to throw out the evil spirits, which are also scared off with loud noises. An alpaca is slaughtered by the *jila*, a native ritual specialist. The *iranta*, as the ceremony is called, is performed to preserve the lands and possessions that might be carried off by the deceased. The ceremony "safeguards and satisfies the earth," *hallpa hapinapak*. The central act is the sacrifice of the alpaca, which is later eaten. A great part of the meat is taken by the *jila* to be distributed among the poor, although he retains the best portions as part of his payment. In a similar fashion, other offerings are made to the earth to pacify it and prevent the soul of the deceased from haunting the living. With the events of the eighth day, the period of mourning is over and the deceased is mentioned as little as possible until the Day of the Dead (November 2), when people go to the cemetery to leave food on the graves. These offerings are given so that the dead will be nourished.

Marriage and the Family

It was not possible for us to validate the existence in Paratía of the so-called *sirvinakuy,* or trial marriage. Instead, there is a traditional union that is valid and grows stronger with the passing of the years. There is, however, some degree of freedom to sever these ties, especially in the early years of marriage when the children are few and are still small. This sanctioned form of union in Paratía differs from the civil or religious marriage common among the mestizos, but it is no less institutionalized.

The parties in these traditional unions are recognized as married by the rest of society and live permanently as such. Their descendants are considered legitimate; rights regarding the property of the *convivientes* (those who live together, i.e., common-law partners) are those of married persons. The freedom to separate has given rise to the idea that this type of marriage involves a trial period, a notion we consider to be false. In most cases, the first marriage endures, and husband and wife have no need of any further ceremonies. If they do resort to a civil or religious marriage, it is done not to legalize the existing arrangement, but to achieve new social advantages or for prestige. In Paratía, civil marriages can be contracted every Thursday at the municipal offices, and as a result these are more numerous than the religious ceremonies performed by the parish priest, who comes only twice a year for the fiestas.

Women are considered marriageable at fifteen and men at seventeen. Until recently parents arranged marriages without considering their children's preferences or obtaining their consent. The bride and groom were presented to each other on the wedding day and locked up in a room; this procedure was called *sonqo khaway* (literally, "to examine the heart"). Outside, the parents and relatives drank until the bride and groom accepted their new status and consented to start a new life together.

In some areas, such as Koarita, endogamic rules which were once very strict still prevail to a certain extent; in Paratía as a whole, some endogamy exists since marriages with strangers and outsiders are rare.

Today the desires of the interested parties are taken into consideration, but parents still have considerable influence in the selection of marriage partners and try by various means to affect their children's decisions. At other times, it is the parents who must accept de facto unions when a son shows up at home with a wife. The announcement of a marriage uses an important term that is difficult to translate. *Iskaykapun* means that what was once one is now two, but that the two are like parts of a whole. The word can be translated literally as "one has duplicated itself" or "now there are two."

When a courtship is pursued in the ideal traditional way, the suitor and his parents go to the girl's house, preferably at night, taking gifts. The quality of the drink (alcohol, beer, and wine), coca, cigarettes, and food they bring will express the esteem in which the future wife's family is held, and at the same time publicize the economic potential of the suitor.

The visit begins with general conversation and small talk; references to the reason for the call are avoided. Nevertheless, after a while, when the guests and hosts are slightly intoxicated, they will discuss their children and their desire to have them marry. This marriage contracted by the parents is called *palabranmantan* ("from words") and confers respect and prestige on the participants. When an agreement over the future wedding has been reached, the drinking is ended. The last cup should be full, with nothing remaining in the bottle. If an excess or shortage occurs, it is better to break the betrothal and not continue with the marriage plans. If the suit has been accepted, and there are no evil omens against it, the bride and groom go to the house of the groom's father to begin their new life. At this time the parents give them alpacas—those allotted to them when they were born as well as those received at their baptism and first haircutting. With these animals and their offspring, the new couple can develop their own herd. Daughters as well as sons receive their animals, and they are included in the joint property of the conjugal unit.

Regardless of the form and model followed by the marriage, the spouses-to-be tend to consult the *jila* beforehand concerning the future of the union and make their decisions in accordance with his advice.

The residence of the newlyweds is patrilocal, and later becomes neolocal when the children build their own house. Although examples are few, other types of matrimonial residence are possible; there are some cases of matrilocality.

Before marriage, both men and women have a great deal of sexual freedom, and their exercise of it is not censured. The children of unmarried girls are raised by their maternal grandparents, and female virginity is not considered a matter of importance. But once a couple is married, the partners must be faithful to each other—although there are those who say that extramarital relationships and infidelity sometimes exist, especially when husbands are away on trading trips. On the other hand, it should be noted that when the men are on trips they try to avoid relationships with other women because they could "suffer bad luck." They believe that serious damage could come to them and their goods if they commit adultery, which is seen as *khencha* (an evil omen). When instances of infidelity do occur, the "other woman" is called *phalla;* the man who maintains relations with a married woman is called *waynayqey.*

Marriage itself is easily dissolved (*t'akanakuy*). If a couple has a disagreement, they may break the contract and return to their parents' homes. If there are children, they are cared for by either partner or by the grandparents. People separated in this way are not severely criticized unless their separations are repeated and frequent, and they have a good chance of entering into a new marriage. Widowers with children rarely remarry, although nothing stops them from doing so. On the other hand, it is difficult for older widows to find a new husband, a situation which does not occur among younger girls, whose access to a second marriage is clear.

The family is organized around parents and children.

When the latter marry, they live in the vicinity of the paternal home, maintaining permanent ties and helping each other with the management of their herds. The authority of the father over his sons—including married ones—the tendency to live in the same neighborhood, and the practice of sharing work are all characteristics of an extended family organization, or great family, in which the male role and male lines of descent and kinship predominate. However, the role of the woman is still important; her opinion counts heavily in family decisions and her option for divorce is evidence enough that she is in no way submissive to her husband. In the absence of the husband, it is she who runs the household, although theoretically the male children assume these responsibilities. Women are in fact the power behind the throne.

Fathers allow their children a good deal of freedom and are not strict with them. Nevertheless, the respect accorded elders is well known. Among siblings there is a certain hierarchy; the younger ones treat the eldest brother, whom they call *kuraq* (the eldest), with deference. If the eldest child is a girl, she relinquishes her position to the brother closest to her in age. The youngest male child remains in his parents' house until they die. His father's herd then becomes his. The older brothers have no right to this herd and have no chance of claiming it.

Some Spanish kin terms have been incorporated into the Paratían kinship system. However, the range of referents for those terms does not always coincide with the range in other societies. There is a strong classificatory tendency in the Paratía kinship system. For example, the sons of brothers (cousins in our kinship system) call each other "brother"; the daughters of sisters (cousins) are also considered sisters. Thus, patterns of deference based on age extend not only to siblings but to cousins as well. Similarly, the brothers and sisters of one's parents (aunts and uncles in our system) are called "father" or "mother."

The spiritual kinship between godparents and godchildren and between *compadres* is very strong and to a certain point resembles that of consanguineal relationships. Godchildren owe respect to their godparents, and the latter should show concern for their godchildren. Godparentship is established at the first haircutting, at baptism, and at marriage. In general, prestigious and wealthy persons within the group are sought as godparents, although sometimes mestizo hacienda owners and even residents of nearby towns, such as Lampa, are asked to take on these roles.

The Learning Process

The small child learns about his culture through informal education and through participating in the society. In Paratía children prepare some types of food, collect cooking fuel, spin and braid ropes, weave slingshots, and above all care for and pasture the alpaca and llama herds. They learn the special skills needed in animal husbandry: supervision of mating, shearing, curing sick animals, slaughtering, and performing the appropriate ceremonies. Later, boys are taught the Andean routes over which they will travel to the lowlands to trade their woven goods, meat, wool, and *charki* for the staples their families need to survive.

In the same manner, the girls are introduced at an early age to spinning and weaving, beginning with simple braids and small cloths. They are often put in charge of fixing meals and looking after their younger brothers and sisters. They begin to learn the secrets required for making ponchos, *llijllas*, blankets, and *aqsu* skirts. The regular absence of the fathers on trading trips and for herding the alpacas creates a situation in which the women, particularly the mothers, spend a great deal of time with their children. The children are therefore enculturated largely under the influence of the mother.

There are two schools in the hamlet of Paratía, one in Kilishani, and another in Koarita. Only the school for boys in Paratía has all the primary grades. Since the girls' school has only one teacher, these two schools have combined so that each teacher can supervise one grade level. It is interesting to note that girls have only recently started to attend school, and parents oppose this practice. Their attitude is understandable if one remembers that not even the boys attend school regularly, because they must help at home and with the herds, and because the school is not yet synchronized with the culture.

To date (1964), two girls have reached the fourth grade of primary school. The goal of those who do go to school is to complete the primary or elementary cycle, but already a few children show a desire to take up higher studies in the secondary schools of Lampa and Juliaca.

Mayor and Governor

A governor appointed by the subprefect of the province of Lampa represents the central government in the district. In addition, each *parcialidad* has a lieutenant governor, called a *teniente*, who assists the governor; the *teniente* helps carry out the governor's political and administrative program, as well as assignments received from higher authorities in the provincial capital, which can have a national character. Further, the governor is present when a person in a position of authority is needed to work with government agencies, such as in sanitation and education campaigns, to capture fugitives, to settle disputes, to collect fees, and even to notify soccer players about forthcoming matches. As can be seen, his functions, above and beyond those generally held by governors, are quite peculiar to the place and are not provided for in any regulations. The positions are honorary and confer great prestige on the officeholder, who sacrifices time and money to fulfill his duties. The length of the term of office varies, depending considerably on those who hold it, as well as on political and administrative fluctuations at the national and departmental levels.

Once a week, always on Thursday, the governor tends to the district's affairs, usually in an office at his home. On this day, the commissioners (*comisarios*) who are the aides of the lieutenant governors, gather, carrying whips decorated with metal strips as symbols of their authority. The governor gives them orders to be transmitted to the lieutenant governors, as well as any other assignments.

The town of Paratía is the seat of the municipal district. It has its own office, which opens its doors on Thursdays, the day reserved for civil marriages and the registration of births and deaths. The mayor elected in the municipal elections of 1963 was the candidate of a party called the Departmental Peasant Front (*Frente Departamental Campesino*). He is a prosperous *hacendado** who has dedicated himself to commerce and is in the process of raising his social status. The walls of the town hall bear graffiti directed against him, including some that are obscene.

A justice of the peace, who is not a lawyer, also reserves Thursdays for public business, although if necessary his services may be engaged any day of the week.

Gods, Saints, and Ayarachi

The supernatural world is vast and interesting, full of ideas, beliefs, prohibitions, fears, and hopes coloring each and every moment of a Paratían's life. Birth, childhood, bartering for food, trade, sickness, marriage, death, animal husbandry, textiles, and even sports are bound up by customs that seem more magical than religious. The people call themselves Catholics, but their Catholicism has some peculiar features. Worship does not extend beyond devotion to the saints themselves, without much attention to the idea that they could be representatives of a higher god. The saints are worshiped, not one omnipotent god; local and family rites count much more than any other religious consideration. Religious services are held in a small chapel with stone walls and a roof of corrugated sheet metal; alongside the chapel is a rather squat tower with a parapet of crudely hewn stone and small, brisk-sounding bells whose complaining tones are heard only on rare occasions.

---

*An *hacendado* is the owner of an estate or ranch (hacienda). [Trans.]

Plaster statues of the saints, kept in small niches, are crudely designed; an art critic would probably find little to admire in them. A few dust-covered oil paintings hang from the walls. When masses are offered, the priest has to be brought from the city of Lampa. For this reason, masses are usually offered only twice a year, but in exceptional cases a zealous worshiper who wants to give thanks for an answered prayer or ask a favor may arrange additional rites.

Until about ten years ago, the town's main fiesta, dedicated to several saints, was celebrated for fifteen days in June, and there were no other fiestas during the year. Today, the fiesta has been split into two dates. The first, always in June, is dedicated to St. Anthony, patron saint of the town; to the Virgin of Carmen; to the Holy Cross; and to the Virgin of Bethlehem. The second fiesta, in October, is to honor the Virgin of the Rosary. According to many people, this division of the fiesta, which was done at the instigation of a parish priest from Lampa, has diminished the splendor and enthusiasm of the original celebration. The *alferados,* sponsors of fiestas, dressed in their finest outfits and accompanied by a host of relatives, friends, and spectators, march toward the chapel carrying ceremonial candles to illuminate the saints' images throughout the celebration. Returning home, they keep vigil through the night until the important day dawns. In the afternoon, after the fiesta mass, the images of the saints and virgins are paraded around the edge of the main plaza. The procession pauses at each corner of the square, where small altars decorated with silks, colored cloths, Peruvian flags, paper flowers, and hundreds of other trinkets have been erected. At each altar the people pray and dance while one of the parishioners, serving as an acolyte, leads them in prayers and hymns.

Following the images, as though they wished to remain apart, are the *ayarachi,* beating their drums with great enthusiasm and imparting a sense of ancient tradition to the proceedings. Here we will pause for a few moments and, in spite of the risk of departing from our main concerns, will attempt a description of the *ayarachi.* (For more details, see Flores-Ochoa 1966.)

The band, or *tropa*, of *ayarachi*, as these musical groups are called, should ideally be composed of twelve musicians. Each one plays a *phuka*, the local name for a *zampoña* or panpipe. These are divided into three types according to size. The longest are called *mama*, the medium ones *lama*, and the shortest *wala*. Sometimes when bands want higher tones they increase the number of musicians, adding smaller pipes known as *suli*. In this case, the band consists of sixteen *ayarachi*.

The *phuku* are also named according to the number of pipes they contain. Those with two rows of six pipes are generically called *ira*, and those with two rows of seven pipes are called *khati*. Melodies are played on the *ira*, while the *khati* play the accompaniment. Adding the size of the *zampoñas* to the number of pipes, the six-pipe instruments are called respectively: *mama ira, lama ira, wala ira,* and *suli ira*. The seven-pipe instruments are called: *mama khati, lama khati, wala khati,* and *suli khati*.

Bands should be composed of numerous pairs of different *zampoñas*, all carefully matched to produce perfect harmony. In the majority of cases there are four instruments from each size category, divided into two *ira* and two *khati*. These pairs are arranged so that a double column of players marches down the street in the following order: *mama, lama, wala,* and *suli* (when there are any), followed by other musicians who maintain the same order. If the musicians play while marching in these columns, there should be a *khati* alongside each *zampoña ira*. When they stop to play, they form a circle, and then *ira* and *khati* *zampoñas* should be facing each other across the circle. All these arrangements are to make certain the music is balanced.

The *phuku* is played with the left hand. At the same time, the right hand beats a drum, or *caja*, which hangs from the shoulder on one side. The drumstick is decorated with multi-colored threads of wool. Here it is interesting to note Cobo's description (1956:270) of the musical instruments:

The most common instrument is the drum they call *huancar;* these, both large and small, are made from a hollow trunk covered at both ends with llama hides, like dry, thin parchment. The large ones are similar to our war drums, but larger and not so well made; the small ones are like a small storage box; and the medium ones resemble our drums. The *huancar* is played with a single stick, which is occasionally decorated with multicolored wool thread. . . .

The *ayarachi*'s costume is quite spectacular, largely because of the enormous crest of feathers worn over the hats. Some of the feathers are from the *suri,* a terrestrial bird (similar to the rhea of the Argentine pampas) which still lives on the vast plains between the high regions of Puno and Moquegua. Other feathers, especially the dyed ones, are acquired in neighboring Bolivia and from the numerous peddlers who frequent the area in search of dried meat and wool.

The feathers of the *phuru* (panache) are attached to a wide band tied around the crown of the fiesta hat. Cobo also mentioned (1956:218, 221) dancers who play *zamponas* and wear plumes on their heads. The *phuru* is fastened to the crown of the hat by the *bandera,* a wide band adorned with metallic threads, glass beads, and even small mirrors. The *bandera* hangs down the back and moves in time with the steps of the musicians. The rest of the costume is the normal fiesta dress. The *ayarachi* members complete their outfit with a long white cloth called a *paño* tied around the neck. This floats behind them like a large cape. From the neck and across the shoulders they hang many *ch'uspa.* Each man usually wears more than thirty or forty, and they practically cover his body. When the men wear *ch'uspa* they do not wear a poncho, and vice versa.

Guided by the first pair of *ayarachi,* the musicians visit the *alferados,* going from house to house. Behind, in a multicolored entourage, their elegantly dressed wives walk in an almost passive manner. The *ayarachi* knock again and again at the doors of the *alferados* until they are invited inside for a special banquet. Great woven cloths are placed on the floor of the patio. On top of these, the visitors are served special dishes prepared with alpaca meat, *chuño,* potatoes, and other foods. The *ayarachi,* who are now called *kuntur* (condors), begin to move their arms, flapping their *paños* like great wings while they hover around the food, moving with steps like those of the great

Using a drumstick held in the right hand, an *ayarachi* player beats out a rhythm on a large drum that hangs on his left side. Simultaneously, he plays a melody on a *zampoña,* or panpipe, which he holds to his mouth with his left hand. The most impressive piece in the *ayarachi* costume is the enormous headdress, which usually includes long feathers from the *suri,* a terrestrial bird living on the highland pampas. A long white cloth is worn in the manner of a cape, and the torso of the musician is covered with thirty or forty *ch'uspa.*

birds. After this preparatory ceremony, they take the food in their mouths without using their hands, as real condors would with their beaks. They fight duels to get as much meat as possible, and then quickly guard it in one of their *ch'uspa*. Through this ritual they say they are feeding the condors, placating them so they will not attack the herds. It should be noted that killing condors is prohibited, and Paratíans are very careful not to break this taboo. The ceremony of giving food to the condors is changing rapidly and at present there are occasions when it is not performed at all, although this omission always provokes criticism.

Leaving the *ayarachi* and returning to religion, we should mention that the people have great faith in the miraculous powers of the Catholic saints. If properly approached, the Paratíans believe, the saints can grant what is asked of them. To support these beliefs they tell of people who visited the chapel, desperately begging for miracles which they claim were then granted.

The people believe very strongly in certain supernatural events, such as the legend of the Child of the Virgin of Bethlehem who escapes from the temple and goes to the area known as Niño Samana (the place where Baby Jesus rests). These nocturnal escapades are known because His slippers, made of immaculate white leather, appear old and dirty, as though used by someone who walked a lot. Furthermore, His small poncho of vicuña wool is covered with seeds from the wild straw of the puna, where the Divine Child runs and plays.

With a faith equal to or exceeding that placed in Christian deities, Paratíans believe in the guardian spirits and protectors of their pantheon, whom they worship every day without waiting for a big fiesta. Whenever the time seems propitious, they call on them. Communication with these spirits is greater and more continuous than with the Catholic saints. The chapel is dusted and swept for the fiesta, but even then the native protective gods—the *apu*, the *principales*—are not forgotten. The *tinka*, *iranta*, and *wilancho*, rituals dedicated to them, are held often and with great devotion. The protecting spirits live in the high and imposing peaks. One should turn to them when asking for good fortune in daily activities, indeed at all times. When Paratíans speak of their gods they say "they are like us" in shape and appearance, but possess great powers. Therefore they are capable of causing harm or ensuring well-being.

Another type of belief is related to the *gentiles*, as the pre-Columbian burial sites are called. The mummies and human remains are greatly respected. They are referred to indiscriminately as *gentiles, awicho* (grandfathers), or *tatala*, and various explanations are given for their origin. Some believe they are "men of the flood," *nawpa runa*, or "very ancient men." Areas where these remains are found are said to be dangerous and should be avoided at all costs since contact with the remains cannot bring anything good. The *awicho* change dwelling places frequently, and this is seen as a demonstration of their power. Their evil emanations can become attached to people who merely pass close by them. The power of the *awicho* causes a wide range of ills in its victims, from simple toothaches to headaches, insanity, seizures, weakness of the arms and legs (*maytu-rapun*), and even, in extreme cases, death. Not only men can be harmed, but also animals, especially domestic animals. If one of these approaches the place where the *tatala* lies, it can die. Some people also believe that those who are struck and killed by lightning are victims of the *tatala*. If a woman sees lights where the *gentiles* live when she urinates nearby, she can become pregnant. When she gives birth, the child is likely to be deformed and usually will die.

The power of the *awicho* can be tamed by the performance of the *pago* or *tinkachi*, certain ceremonies accompanied by offerings which can be held at any time or on a regular basis with the *tinka*, a sprinkling of drops of alcohol on the floor. When carnival is celebrated, Paratíans prepare boiled *kañiwa* and *kinuwa* in the form of *pesque* or *k'ispiño* and other soft dishes that do not need to be chewed. With great thoughtfulness, they remember that the *abuelitos* (ancestors, grandparents), owing to their age and the poor condition of their teeth, are not able to eat hard food; thus, in order to keep them happy, they try to avoid such foods. Once these ceremonies have begun, it is dangerous to discontinue them for any reason since even involuntary forgetfulness is not pardoned. This happened to one old man who presented offerings every year to the *awicho* during carnival. One year, through negligence, he forgot the ritual and from that moment misfortunes began to afflict him. One by one, he lost all his animals, and before a year had passed he was struck by a bolt of lightning.

In the main houses there are altars where the male heads of households, in the presence of the women, officiate as priests in carrying out the *pago* and other propitiatory ceremonies of the family cult. The altars, called *mesa* and *pikota*, are made of rocks and mud. They are like miniature rooms, but not even fifteen centimeters above the ground. The offerings are buried inside them. If the house does not have one of these altars, a substitute is made of stones placed in a circle. Another offering site, usually called *pikota*, is made of a cylindrical stone stuck in the middle of the corrals. Around it fertility rites are held during carnival. Offerings consist of pieces of llama fat, coca leaves, bottles of alcohol, cigarettes, branches of *wallakaya*, incense, caramels, dishes of *kinuwa*, and *kañiwa* in the form of *k'ispiño*. Everything burnt together makes up the *pago*. The *wilancho* is another ceremony involving the sacrifice of alpacas and llamas and the use of their blood. This ceremony is quite common during the fiestas accompanying the building of houses.

Various prohibitions are highly respected because breaking them can cause serious ailments. When a man goes on a trip he should not kill any animal, either wild or domestic. This restriction also applies to his family, even to the extent that animals cannot be sold to a buyer who might slaughter them for his own consumption. At no time do the people eat domestic fowl, because they cannot kill them. They are raised only to produce eggs or to be traded alive. In this way, the natives avoid seeing them die and do not have to be ashamed and repent later on. No wild animals of any kind should be raised because it is *khuya*, bad luck. Another prohibition prevents the killing of vicuñas. The worst possible personal and family harm will be suffered by anyone who commits this act. Neither do they kill condors, for to do so would be to seek the death of a relative. Skunks and owls should also not be killed, although sometimes merely seeing one is enough to cause a relative's death.

Ceremonial activities control every moment of a Paratían's life, and there is no single stage of life, whether important or insignificant, that is not preceded by a *pago.* When considering marriage, the people consult the spirits to see if destiny favors the union. When a child is to be born, or if they want to help with the birth, they resort to a *pago.* An *iranta* takes place on the death of a relative, among other things to forestall the death of more family members. Sicknesses are treated by conjuration, offering sacrifices on the *mesa.* During the days of *saruchi,* or mating, once the family is gathered together in the alpaca corral, they perform the *iranta* to ask for a good year—that the pastures may grow; that there be many offspring, especially those with white wool; and that the animals shall not die in large numbers. Upon changing herding areas (*ahijaderos*), before installing themselves in the new residence, the herders offer a *pago* in the corral. Before shearing the alpacas they also petition the spirits. When the day comes when new animals might be born, offerings are again given. If lightning should kill an alpaca, this is interpreted as a sign that there must be a new *pago.* Another animal should be sacrificed so that no more will die and so the next misfortune will not strike a person or a house.

Before the men set out on a trading journey, an *iranta* is performed over two small cloths, or *unkuña,* containing coca leaves, branches of *wallakaya,* and llama fat. The natives implore the high peaks, the *principales,* that no misfortune befall them on their way and that they return home safely. Then, the head of the family or the man of the group directs the ceremony (it cannot be a woman, not even the mother of the family). Drops of alcohol are scattered on the ground while the names of the tutelary mountains are invoked. Then the leader proceeds to drink, followed by the others who are going on the trip, continuing with the boys if they are not grown up, and, only at the end, the women. The *unkuña* are stored with care until the travelers come home. Then, in another ceremony, the returned travelers will burn the contents of the *mesa* to thank the *apu* for granting them a safe journey. Also, before engaging in commercial transactions, the herders are accustomed to conducting a *pago*. When a house is built, before digging the foundations, they perform an *iranta;* and when the house is completed, they bless the walls with a *wilancho*. There are even athletes who call upon the *principales* when their teams are going to take part in a competition.

When the people of Paratía feel that their personal powers need bolstering, they go to specialists—to healers in cases of common illnesses like *muro p'acha* (a swelling of the eyes attributed to not wearing a hat) or *lleqti* (blisters on the lips); and to sorcerers for ailments supernaturally caused. The difference between the two is very subtle, and most of the time the same person combines the two specialties. Only men can dedicate themselves to these activities. Although women can perform certain cures, they do not assume the functions of the specialists.

These practitioners of spells and cures are indiscriminately called *jila* or *tata paqo*. Their powers can be acquired through formal training under a master who receives money in exchange for his teaching, sometimes as much as three thousand soles (in 1964). This training is known as *makin aysarin,* "the transmission by hand," which refers to the transfer of the powers and secrets of the profession. Other *paqo* acquire their powers through a supernatural sign—generally something extraordinary like being struck by lightning—which confers the privilege of curing patients directly or of using exorcisms.

Paratíans speak of fabulous cures by a *paqo* who has a "good hand," or *allin mikisitu,* of dead or dying persons who were returned to life by the right payment to the earth. Using various procedures, the *paqo* assist at childbirth to ensure that the birth will proceed smoothly. For example, they unwind balls of wool which women wound during the three months prior to the birth, and then they choose a few threads to twist in the opposite direction. If difficulty at childbirth is presumed to stem from the fact that the woman heated a toasting pan (*hiqi*) without using it, this receptacle is placed on her back and moved in a circular motion. So that the malady will not return, a piece of the placenta is roasted and given to the woman to drink in a maté, together with pieces of fingernail and burnt hairs.

Patients cannot change specialists once they have placed themselves in their care. No one would agree to treat them for fear that the "powers would cross" and thus be lost. They say: "When one puts one's hand (power) where another has placed his, one might lose the hand (power)."

The *jila* are truly important in the people's lives. Prospective husbands go to them to consult about the likelihood of a happy marriage. According to the answers the *jila* reads in the coca leaves, the interested parties decide whether to proceed with their plans. The *jila* are consulted on business matters and the loss of animals. To obtain a good shearing, it is thought to be expedient for the *jila* to perform a *pago*. The ceremony on the eighth day following a death should be directed by the *jila*. The offering on the death of an animal killed during a storm also requires intervention by a *jila*. The *jila* are feared, but they are not held in very high regard and may even be hated. The Paratíans feel they are capable of causing great harm. Although none of them claim the ability to produce evil, the people think that if they can cure illnesses they must also be able to cause them.

Siren and Illa

The folklore of Paratía is quite interesting and includes narratives about supernatural figures, tales of tiny, clever beings, and stories which explain the natural world. Although many narratives contain European elements, they have been adapted to the local setting.

Among the principal traditional narratives is one about a siren who appears in the late afternoon on an enormous rock in the middle of the Paratía River, southeast of the village. She is a woman with a white complexion and red hair who attracts the men with her sweet song. Those who hear her must not pay any heed, for to do so would bring them under her spell and could cause incurable insanity. The story of the siren is strengthened by accounts of experiences with sirens that some Paratíans claim to have had. Sometimes the siren is useful, and helpful, too, because she can temper stringed instruments left for her in the evening. The next day they are magnificently tuned and produce excellent melodies, "almost like those on the radio." In exchange for these services one leaves silver coins or ancient Peruvian coins of nickel silver. The music from instruments tuned by the siren has the virtue of producing strange sensations in listeners, especially in women, who can then be easily seduced. Cases are cited of musicians who had their instruments perfectly tuned by the siren.

On nights when the moon is full, it is said to be possible to see a black bull on the waters of certain lagoons in the highlands. His hide glistens and reflects the light of the stars. This legend is known as "The Magic Bull."

On some nights in the village of Paratía the hurried trot of a troop of mules can be heard. They are pulling a cart bearing a coffin. To hear and perhaps see the animals is a sign that an acquaintance or family member will soon die.

People also tell a story about a bet between the fox and Patrón Santiago (St. James) over who could make the most noise. To settle the matter, all the foxes got together and slapped the ground with their tails. When it was Patrón Santiago's turn, he used his sword to cut a swath, producing a bolt of lightning and a tremendous noise that terrified the foxes. Since that day the foxes run for shelter whenever it thunders.

There is a pretty story about the *luli*, a very small bird, and the condor, the king of the heights. The two enter into hostilities, and the *luli*, in spite of his small size and physical disadvantage, conquers the powerful condor. This narrative can be interpreted as the victory of the weak over the strong. The legend is as follows:

There is a small green bird with a large beak, similar to the hummingbird, who knows everything and is called *luli*.
The condor had stolen the daughter of an *hacendado*, taking her to his nest. Desperate, her father told the *luli*, who knows everything,

that he could have his daughter in marriage if he could rescue her. The *luli* was able to save her and took her home.

The condor, unable to find the girl, immediately suspected the *luli*, because he knew everything and thus was the only one capable of rescuing her. So the condor went to the *luli*'s house. The *luli* lives in a small hole, and so the condor could not enter. The condor urged the *luli* to come out and return the woman to him. The *luli* answered that he was preparing to do just that. In the meantime, he was busy sharpening a penknife with a rock. He said to the condor, "I am putting on my shoes." Every time the condor inquired, the *luli* answered that he was putting on another article of clothing. The condor was waiting for him with his mouth open wide over the entrance to the *luli*'s house, ready to swallow him when he came out. When the penknife was very sharp, the *luli* came out with such force that he went all the way to the entrails of the condor, destroying him. Cutting open the condor's stomach he came out, free to marry the *hacendado*'s daughter.

The condor is feared and there is some animosity toward him because he can attack the herds. At the same time there is a taboo against killing him. Nevertheless, the story shows that another, smaller bird, who may represent man himself, is capable of destroying the condor.

Another example of the oral literature, although not very well known, especially among the young people, is the myth about the origin of the alpacas. The version we present here has several elements, and as far as possible the translation preserves the meaning it would have in Quechua.

They say that in *Pacha Paqariy* (The Dawn Epoch) there was a man who lived in *Kay Pacha* (This World) and a beautiful woman who lived in *Ukhu Pacha* (The Inner World). She had herds with many alpacas, but they were attacked and eaten by the *anka* [a small eagle]. She was unable to protect them because she could not fight with the *anka*. She saw that in *Kay Pacha* there were also herds of alpacas and that the man who took care of them could fight and defend them from other beasts. Noting this, the father of the woman of *Ukhu Pacha* permitted her to marry the man because he knew how to fight against the *anka* and so could protect the herds. The father allowed his daughter to leave with all his alpacas so they could reproduce in This World. With them, occupying a preferred position, went a tiny alpaca.

This was the *illa,* which had to be carefully watched over and carried in their arms, always guarded and protected, while they went from one place to another.

One day the woman returned to *Ukhu Pacha* to visit her father, who was alone. She left the herds of alpacas in the care of her husband, charging him to be very careful with the *illa* and always carry her in his arms. The husband did not want to take the trouble, and, overcome with laziness, he killed the tiny alpaca to free himself from the bother of caring for her.

When the wife returned to our world, she discovered, to her complete astonishment and indignation, that the *illa* was missing. She asked for it, and upon learning that it had been killed, she became furious; full of anger, she decided to return to her own world. Walking toward a spring, she started to return to *Ukhu Pacha,* followed by all the alpacas. The man, seeing her go, was full of fear, and tried to prevent the animals from approaching the spring. But he was only able to stop a few animals from following the woman to the underworld. Since that time, the herds of alpacas grazing on the pastures of the earth have been few, and this is the reason they like to graze on marshy sites where springs are found; they still want to return to *Ukhu Pacha.*

This story is an interesting example of the rich traditions in oral literature. It also suggests the presence of elements that appear to be of pre-Columbian origin. The ancient Peruvians divided the world into three parts: *Hanan Pacha,* or The Upper World; *Kay Pacha,* or This World; and *Ukhu Pacha,* or The Inner World. The story deals with two of these worlds. In *Kay Pacha* there are men, animals, plants, and, in general, all living beings. *Ukhu Pacha* is the resting place of the dead, of the spirits who communicate with this world by means of the *paqarina:*

Between the Inner World and This World there is communication through holes in the earth's surface—caverns, caves, and volcanic craters; also the depths of lakes or places where water gushes out, springs, and brooks. All of these points of contact with the Inner World are what the ancient Peruvians called "Pacarina." [Valcárcel 1946b:137]

The *puho,* or spring, in the story is a *paqarina* through which the alpacas emerged to the surface world and through which they also returned to *Ukhu Pacha* as punishment for the idleness of the man and his murder of the *illa*. The *illa* is believed to have the power to vouchsafe the welfare of the alpacas, and any misdeed against her has direct consequences for the reproduction of the herds. The *illa*, at present, is represented by an amulet used in ceremonies concerned with the fertility of the animals. It can be found in shapes representing animals, made of white stone or metal, or it can even be a simple rock of a whimsical shape found in the countryside.

The *illa* were already present in the magico-religious activities of pre-Columbian Peru and were considered amulets, as Rowe (1946:297) indicates, citing Cobo, Arriaga, and González.

CHAPTER 3

HERDERS, WEAVERS,
AND TRADERS

FOR THE PEOPLE who live at these altitudes, their daily existence is a permanent and continuous challenge which must be met with perseverance, cunning, and great ingenuity. There are few places in the world where the habitat is more inhospitable. The cold and the altitude are obstacles that have been conquered by the Andean inhabitants, who have learned to use almost all the resources offered by the environment. The large, grassy areas are good pastures for the lamoids native to the Andes, and it is through herding that the people survive.

The principal property in Paratía consists of herds of camelids, from which people obtain everything required to satisfy their basic needs. They do not make pottery because they do not possess the necessary technical knowledge; nor do they practice agriculture, in part because the area is unsuitable for cultivation and in part because their culture is limited by their pastoral way of life. Poor soils, heavy snows, and freezing nights are not favorable to food crops. To obtain such items, Paratíans must engage in an intense and interesting trade with the agricultural villages in the areas known as the *bajíos*, or lowlands.

Alpacas and llamas are herded. Other animals introduced by the Europeans, such as sheep and cattle, are not abundant. This lack of penetration is due not so much to an inability to adapt as to the unwillingness of herders above 4,300 meters to make these animals a more important part of their pastoral activities.

The *alpaca, pako,* or *pakocha* (the animal is referred to by all of these terms, the first preferred by those who speak Spanish and the last two by natives) was domesticated by the ancient Peruvians, the ancestors of the very herders who now live on the Peruvian Altiplano. According to Murra (1964:76–77):

As a result of the investigations by Cardich, we have proof that lamoids were already being hunted 8,000 years ago. The date of domestication is still unknown, but from the remains excavated on the coast, it can be deduced that in the mountains domestication already existed in the Chavín Epoch, 1000 B.C. According to Junius Bird, the major inducement for domestication was the growing interest of coastal weavers in the acquisition of wool. However, it is conceivable that the guanaco and alpaca were tamed in their natural habitat by hunters who in the course of 5,000 years learned much about their behavior. The area around Titicaca, where there is the largest concentration of domesticated as well as wild species, has been suggested as the site of this domestication. Troll and other geographers find a close correlation between the ecology of the puna and the distribution of domesticated camelids: "in a biological sense, llamas and alpacas belong to a puna biotype . . ."; if these animals are found in other areas, such as Chile or Ecuador, Troll considers them only marginal, "artificially" introduced by the Inca State.

Alpacas are lamoids that live in places above 4,000 meters. Of all the domesticated animals native to the Americas, they are the most successfully adapted to life at this altitude. Among their favorable physical qualities are a normal pulse rate between 54 and 100 beats per minute, a respiratory rate of 20 to 40 breaths per minute, and blood containing approximately 20 million red corpuscles per cubic millimeter, along with a fast coagulation rate. One disadvantage is an excessive dependency on water which confines them within strict environmental limits (Gilmore 1950:429ff.). Thanks to a split lip, alpacas can eat short, tough grasses easily. The gestation period is 11½ months and birth comes in the rainy season, between December and March when the mothers are able to produce more milk because of the greater abundance of grass (Moro 1964:33). From head to tail, alpacas measure approximately 150 to 175 centimeters and in height they are between 80 and 90 centimeters. Their fleece sometimes hangs to the ground. Their ears are about 12 to 15 centimeters long. The head is of medium size with big, constantly growing teeth and large eyes. They have five teats, four of which are functional and produce from 15 to 500 cubic centimeters of milk every twelve hours (Moro 1964:33). Female alpacas can be fertile for as long as 15 to 17 years, although the animals are slaughtered when they are no longer economically profitable. This age may vary in different areas but it is usually seven years. Alpacas are sometimes allowed to live for nine or ten years; they are then killed for their meat, leather, and fat.

There are two main breeds of alpaca, distinguished mainly by the quality of their wool. The *suri* produces a finer wool that is heavier, longer, and shinier, but it has the disadvantage of producing weak offspring susceptible to disease and changes in climate and food. The *wakayo* (sometimes called *wakaya*) has a rougher, short wool with less sheen. In compensation for this deficiency, the *wakayo* has greater resistance to diseases and climatic changes and a greater ability to digest short, tough grass. In addition, since the offspring are born with more wool and are better able to withstand the cold, the *wakayo* have a lower mortality rate. This breed is also called *chhaku** because of the coarse quality of its wool.

The alpacas are greatly loved by the Paratíans. Sometimes the animals are given names and become pets, trailing after their owners. There are several ways of classifying and recognizing the animals, and each herder can always pick out his own. The principal categories refer to colors and their patterning. The more common colors are *yurak,* or white; *yana,* or black; *pako,* a light brown; *chumpi,* or dark brown, almost chocolate; and *oqhe,* or gray. *Alqa* refers to a combination of colors on the animal, a large dark area (black, brown, or gray, for example) surrounded by a light color. The eyes are also a differentiating trait. Those with light eyes (almost blue) are known as

---

*Dr. Flores-Ochoa clarifies this term as follows: "It is applied to an animal with lots of wool that hangs down the sides and also over the face. It can also be used for dogs." [Trans.]

misti ñawi. Those alpacas with extra toes are called *phorqa* and
are highly valued because they are thought to be lucky.

As mentioned earlier, alpaca offspring are always born
during the day, and the newborns are called *tuwi.* After two or
more years, when they become sexually mature, they are called
ankota. The terms reserved for the adult male are *k'achi* and
allpaka orqo; a female with offspring is called *china mama.*

The mortality rate of young alpacas is rather high, and the
number of births is low because many adult males are sterile
and females frequently abort. As a result, the growth rate of
the herds is slow, and diseases often diminish them even more.
All this naturally tends to provoke anxiety and uncertainty
among the herd owners, since the herds are their major source
of subsistence goods. The men of Paratía resort to magic to
calm their fears and, without exaggeration, it can be said that
there is no activity in their daily lives not surrounded by practices designed to control "luck" and enlist the aid of the spirits
of the mountains and the earth.

The magical ceremonies are intensified during carnival and
continue until the celebration of Easter. During this period,
which begins in January, people are busy with mating the alpacas and caring for the newborns. We should repeat that magical activities intensify during the season of *pujllay* (carnival).

Both male and female alpacas reach sexual maturity at
about two years of age. Herders pick mates for some animals
and control the entire process. The males are put in corrals
along with the females for the *saruchi,* or mating, an event
mentioned with great interest and enthusiasm; singing, dancing, and general gaiety abound. However, these festive activities are not exempt from anxiety since destiny might be cruel.

The females are pregnant when they shun the males and
no longer respond to their advances. The females are then
gathered into a special herd and marked on their backs with
pieces of colorful yarn. This separation protects the females
from assaults by the males and makes it easier to care for the
young. Females may have from five to seven pregnancies and
are sexually receptive again within twenty-four hours after giving birth.

The herd of females and offspring, watched over by special caretakers who guard the young from pumas and foxes, is maintained until the offspring are weaned at approximately eight months. This protection is supplemented with magic—small woven bags, *wallkita,* containing special herbs, are hung around the necks of the animals to keep them from danger and safeguard their health.

The herds of male alpacas are given some liberty. They are free from continuous care and protection, although from time to time they are glanced at to be sure they will return to their corrals, or *iphiña,* in the afternoon. Males who are not good studs or whose excessive sexual appetite needs to be curbed are prevented from reproducing by cutting off their testicles with a knife or, commonly, by biting them off and extracting them in one's mouth. Castrated males may remain in the same herds with the females.

There are also herds in which a special class of animal is raised, specifically white alpacas. These animals are preferred because their wool is more valuable. They are also a sign of prestige, showing that their owners are careful people and good herders.

Herds are moved from one pasture, or *ahijadero,* to another on a seasonal basis in search of good and abundant grass with plenty of water. There are rainy-season pastures and dry-season pastures. The latter are used from June to December; in December the herds are moved to the rainy-season pastures, which are at lower altitudes than the dry-season ones (Chart 1). During the summer rains, the grass grows well, but at times the earth is covered with snow and the alpacas cannot find food. For this reason the *ahijaderos* at higher altitudes are reserved for the winter or dry season. In years when there is little rain, and therefore poor grass, the alpacas may die of *tege,* emaciation. The meat from such animals cannot be used since it spoils easily and has a bad taste.

This system of herding in *ahijaderos* has created the need for each family to have several homes, a principal one and other temporary ones in the *ahijaderos.* The main residence is located somewhere between the summer and winter pastures.

Chart 1. Annual Cycle of Pastoral Activities in Paratía

		August	September	October	November	December	January	February	March	April	May	June	July
	MONTH* / SEASON	Dry —	Windy —	Great dryness	←	Rainy and snowy →				Dry →		← Frosts →	
PASTORAL ACTIVITIES	Location of Herds	Pasturing in the higher elevations			← Pasturing in the lower zones, the pampas →						Pasturing in the higher elevations		
	Key Tasks	Weaving — Spinning				Mating — Shearing				Curing	Slaughter — Making *charki*		
	Complementary Tasks	Weaving — Spinning					Spinning					Weaving — Spinning	
	Forms of Residence	In the *cabañas* (family dispersed)				In the *estancias* (family concentrated)						In the *cabañas* (family dispersed)	
	Altitude of Residence	4,400 meters or more above sea level				4,400 meters or less above sea level					Climbing to areas more than 4,400 meters above sea level		
INTERZONAL TRADE	Product	Corn	Corn, Potatoes	Wheat, Barley			Figs, Apples, Peaches					Corn, Potatoes, Barley	
	Region	Valleys of Arequipa	Huanca fair	Arequipa and Puno			Valleys of Moquegua					Arequipa and Puno	
SALE	Wool and Skins	Valleys of Moquegua and Arequipa								Lampa, Santa Lucia, Juliaca, Cabanillas			
	Fresh Meat	Valleys of Moquegua and Arequipa					Valleys of Moquegua						
PASTORAL CEREMONIES	Rites	*Wilancha*						*Pago*					
	Motive	Pastures					For fertility of alpacas and llamas; Carnival						
CATHOLIC FIESTAS				Virgin of the Rosary								Virgin of Carmen and St. Anthony	

The care and management of the alpacas requires the participation of almost the entire family, men and women, children and adults. Everyone knows how to take care of the animals, but the main daily responsibilities, such as taking them in and out of the corrals, fall to the children. The father and other adult males in the family are busy selling the wool and cloth, and the women are occupied with weaving. The herds are let loose in the pastures in the morning and return or are brought home to the corrals in the afternoon. They are driven by whistles, shouts, and by cracking whips and ropes. The animals are not punished or mistreated because the Paratíans claim they would run away to inaccessible places and retrieving them would mean a lot of effort and an exhausting chase. The herders are able to recognize each of their alpacas individually, and as a result they do not use a branding system. The colored threads attached to animals' ears during the *pujllay* are mainly expressions of the owners' esthetic sense, combined with a bit of magic.

Of the various products derived from alpaca herding, the primary one is wool. The average production per alpaca is around three kilograms if the animal is shorn every two years and half that amount if it is shorn annually.* The majority of the herders shear their animals once a year. However, they will occasionally shear before the time is up if they urgently need to sell wool in order to buy consumer goods. Pastoralists with larger herds, and most mestizo *hacendados*, shear every two years because this practice is said to yield more wool; the wool is also heavier then and has longer fibers.

Shearing is done in the summer, around Christmastime; although it is sometimes begun earlier, it does not take place later than February or March. The day set for the *rutuchi* (shearing) is a very busy one for the family. From grandparents to grandchildren, everyone joins in a fiesta complete with music, plenty of good food, a lot of drink, and a generally joyful atmosphere. Shearing is very much like the harvest among farmers—hence all the merriment that surrounds it.

---

*Moro (1964:33) says that annual shearings produce from three to five kilos and biennial shearings from four to eight kilos.

According to the Paratíans, shearing should begin at the head, continue along the neck, and finish with the extremities. The fibers from the legs, the chest, and the neck, called *chichillinkuna* and *kanchokuna,* are of inferior quality and are considered suitable for making ropes, cords, and coarse fabrics. For shearing, the people use large scissors and metal knives that have been sharpened on flat rocks. Sometimes they use pieces of broken glass. Cuts and wounds from the shearing process are treated with alcohol and ashes.

After wool, the second important alpaca product is meat, which is definitely a complementary benefit since the animals are not raised exclusively as a source of meat. Paratíans eat the meat of animals that have died of natural causes or by accident, or those killed because of old age. They eat fresh meat, but they also sometimes salt and dehydrate it, producing *charki.* The fat, approximately four to six kilos per animal, is eaten and used both in trade and for magical purposes. The use depends on the degree of solidity; the finest, of course, is consumed.

Alpaca hides are used to make rope, *tientos* (thin ropes that bind the roofs), and sandals. When the hide still has wool on it, it is used for mattresses and pillows.

People also herd another camelid, the llama. This animal does not have the same importance and does not arouse the same degree of interest as the alpaca. Llamas are raised as a supplement to alpacas. Although the two are pastured together, care is taken to separate the male from the female herds.

The physical characteristics of llamas are similar to those of alpacas. They are a little bigger, heavier, and covered with a rougher wool, which is thick, strong, and greasy (Gilmore 1950:433ff.). Their meat is used for domestic consumption, mostly in the form of *charki.* The fat is used in medicine and magic, and the hides serve the same purposes as those of the alpacas. Both ruminants provide a large proportion of the fuel used in the herders' kitchens: their sun-dried feces, in the form of *wayk'una,* are the principal source of fuel. This is collected in the early winter and stored for later use.

Llamas are raised primarily because of their usefulness as pack animals. Beginning at two or three years (*ankota*), they are trained for this work. The herders start them carrying a few kilos, and the weight is progressively increased until they reach a total capacity that can be up to forty kilos. On long trips lasting as many as thirty consecutive days, they carry less weight—between twenty-five and thirty kilos—and travel fifteen to twenty kilometers a day in ten-hour marches. In areas where food is scarce, the llamas can go four or five days without eating, according to their drivers. One man alone can control a drove of twenty to thirty animals; the most capable drivers can manage even larger droves, up to forty or fifty animals.

The herders do not interfere with the mating of llamas, which takes place from December through April. The births follow approximately eleven months later. The young suckle for four or five months, very rarely until eight. They are then separated from their mothers. Some males are castrated for better meat and wool production, although the Paratíans prefer to leave them intact so they can be used to carry cargo.

The male llama is called *tatala;* the female is known as *china mama.* The ears of both are decorated with colored threads called *t'ika* (flowers) during carnival.

The main difficulties faced by the herders are sterility of the animals, abortions, the periodic droughts of the Altiplano, lack of suitable pastureland, and diseases such as *sarna* (scabies). *Sarna* is caused by mites that settle in the upper layers of the skin and lead to the formation of thick scabs that can sometimes be almost two fingers high; these produce a loosening of the skin and can weaken the animal, which is then susceptible to other potentially fatal diseases. *Sarna* is most dangerous in very young and very old llamas. Of at least equal, and perhaps greater, importance is diarrhea caused by *Clostridium wilchi* (Plan Regional 1959), which decimates the llama offspring, killing as many as 50 to 90 percent of those under three months old.

In Paratía's "low" zones, at around 4,200 meters, it is possible to find a few herds of ordinary sheep in areas near cultivated fields. These sheep produce little wool and are mainly used to supply meat for the mestizos and the towns of Lampa, Palca, Santa Lucía, and perhaps even Juliaca. The herds are small and do not rival those of the alpacas because the herders attach little importance to them. The situation is similar for cows and oxen, which provide meat for the same towns and for the coastal cities. There are few horses, and these are small and shaggy, but strong and hardy. The natives are good horsemen who like to attract attention; they see themselves as gentlemen when riding on these nags. Sheep, cattle, and horses are owned by mestizo landowners and acculturated Indians (*cholos*) who wish to show their identification with the *misti* in this way.

It should be stressed that the ownership of alpaca and llama herds is of paramount importance for the people of the Paratía cordillera. Although we made no detailed studies of property, distribution of pastures, and the number and quality of the herds, we did note that there were both wealthy pastoralists and poor ones. We were told that some natives have herds of three to five hundred animals, with herds of white *suri* separated from the rest and more than one *ahijadero* for each season. At the other extreme are the *wahcha*, or people without herds, who seek the protection of a rich person (*qhapah*), or attach themselves to an hacienda as salaried herders with the right to maintain a few alpacas. In the middle are those with herds of around seventy or more animals. Owning a herd is the most important concern of the natives because possession of a herd is vital to raising and supporting a family. When a son is born, the father gives a few alpacas to the newborn and keeps them in the son's name. From that moment they are referred to as the boy's animals. The offspring from this small group increase the size of his "herd"; he also receives additional animals at his Catholic baptism and more at his first haircutting, thanks to his godparents. In this way, the future property of the child is accumulated. His herd is turned over to him when he comes of age and marries. In general, boys have more alpacas than girls because it is assumed that girls will eventually marry a man with a sufficiently large herd to permit them to raise a family.

Spinning and Weaving

In Paratía the wool from the herds is woven into a variety of goods to exchange in trade with farmers. It is also made into garments and other cloth for daily use. Obviously, weaving and animal husbandry are highly intertwined and closely connected with trade.

Before weaving can take place, the fleece is spun into long threads. Everyone in Paratía, no matter what sex or age, takes part in spinning wool. From early childhood, individuals begin to carry their spindles with them; women keep their hands busy with the spindle while talking to relatives or taking care of children. People spin while traveling, while taking a break from other work, while watching the herds or coming home from school. The older people, no matter how incapacitated they may be, spend hour after hour spinning. It would not be an exaggeration to say that the entire life cycle involves spinning, since people of all ages engage in this task whenever they can. Hands are always ready for spinning.

Wooden spindles (*kanti*) are acquired in the neighboring towns during fairs. The size of the spindle varies, depending on who uses it. Spindles are made of a rod of sanded wood inserted through the center of a wooden disc that serves as a counter-weight. The disc also collects the thread and controls the speed. The tip of the spindle usually spins on a broken piece of pottery or fragments of pottery utensils. It is interesting to note that many individuals turn the spindle counterclockwise, while the mestizos spin in the opposite direction. Finer threads go through two consecutive spinnings. The first, called *phuskay*, leaves rough, irregular threads; the second, *tapa*, gives stronger, thinner threads. When the spinning is finished, the wool is wound into skeins, or *juñi*, which vary in size and weight.

The fabrics manufactured for trade are generally made with undyed wool, preferably black, white, gray, and what is called "alpaca colored" wool, although some ponchos are dyed gray or *nogal*, a light brown popular with the mestizos. When the Paratíans weave garments for themselves—ponchos for the men, *llijllas* for the women, and a variety of other items—they

Weaving with the ground loom is women's work. While men use the upright loom of European origin to weave homespun, women are the true specialists in the craft of weaving. They make blankets, bags, and simple garments, such as the poncho shown above, to be traded by the men on their commercial journeys, but they also produce the elegant *llijllas* and ponchos worn by Paratíans at fiestas.

color the material with mineral dyes obtained at fairs in nearby towns or from traveling salesmen. To fix the colors, they use lemon juice and even whole lemons, although some people use lemon salt (*sal de limón*) bought in stores and pharmacies in the towns. These dyes are not very powerful, and they fade when exposed to the sun and the rain, and after washing. Since the colors "leave," as they say, people usually wear their clothing inside out.

Weaving is basically a feminine occupation. Women weave trade items such as sacks, blankets, ponchos, and shawls. They also weave the beautiful men's multicolored ponchos, as well as the decorated *llijlla* and *aqsu* skirts, the beautiful *qompi* blankets, and other smaller items such as the *wayaka* (a tiny sack) and the *ch'uspa*. Men weave very little, and when they do they limit themselves to making a fabric known as *bayeta* (homespun), which is used for trade or for their own clothing. They also make cords, rope, sandals, slings, and belts.

There are two kinds of loom (*away*), one horizontal and one vertical. The first, undoubtedly indigenous to this area and probably of pre-Columbian origin, is similar to those used in the department of Cuzco. The length and width of the material is determined from the moment the warp is strung, made taut by two wooden rollers, *awaqaspikuna*. One roller is tied to two wooden nails, or *takarpu*. The other, which winds the material during the work, is also tied to a pair of *takarpu* with cords. These cords keep the material taut and are loosened as the fabric is rolled up until the two *awaqaspikuna* are so close that to finish the weaving a new wooden roller, the *wasanchana qaspi*, must be used as the warp rod.

Between the warp threads are the *tokoro*, small bars which separate them and through which the woof threads run. The *miñu akchunita* serves as a shuttle. The warp is raised or lowered by means of the heddle, or *illawa qaspi*, and the *tokoro*, a warp rod with threads wound to form loops that make certain threads of the warp go up and down. The woof is propelled by means of flat, polished pieces of wood called *wichurqatito* and *rok'enka*, aided by the *wichuña*, a pick made of bone from a deer or other animal. This instrument is highly valued and is passed from generation to generation. An owner will consent to part with it only with great reluctance.

The looms described above are used by the women. When the men weave, they use vertical European-style looms which are provided with various pedals to manipulate the warp threads and crosspieces (Mishkin 1946:431–432). They also have warp rods that turn freely so the weaver can produce materials of varied lengths, adding to the warp threads for as long as he wishes. The *bayeta* made on these looms is cut and sewn to create some of the men's and women's clothing.

The average woman, seated on a *mast'aña*, a circular straw mat, weaves for many hours during the day. She starts working at dawn, pausing only to cook, take care of the children, or perform other routine chores. The coldness of cloudy, windy days does not prevent her from working outside; her weaving cannot be done indoors because the huts are small and even colder than the outdoors. The dry season is a perfect time for weaving, though occasionally the strong sun can cause sunstroke. The beginning of the rains and snowstorms is the sign that it is best to start working on something else.

The good weavers, esteemed for the quality of their fabrics and their speed in making them, are commissioned to work for other people. Women who do not have enough wool to keep themselves busy weaving will also work for others, receiving payment in wool plus food and coca. With this wool they can weave cloth that their husbands will later trade.

The garments and fabrics made for trade have no decorations. At most, the weaver may alternate threads of different natural colors—in the bags, black and white threads are combined to make broad vertical stripes. The ponchos for the lowlands people, or *misti poncho,* are of a solid color, sometimes with small red or green lines.

Embellishment reaches fantastic dimensions when the Paratíans weave for themselves; even in the *bayeta* for clothing, shades of white, dark brown, black, and gray are combined in striking geometric designs. But their artistic skills are most spectacular in their traditional garments—ponchos, *aqsu, qompi* blankets, *llijlla,* jackets, and *unkuña.*

Although there are common decorative patterns, each artist has a certain margin of freedom in which to add personal touches to her work. There is always informal competition among weavers, since some fabrics are more highly esteemed. The natives are able to recognize the hand that produced a certain weaving by the quality of the finished item as well as the design and colors. The best weavers achieve a superior status and enjoy much prestige. Some women specialize in a certain kind of weaving, even though they can do the others as well.

The decorative motifs can be grouped into four principal categories: geometric, zoomorphic, phytomorphic, and anthropomorphic. In the first there are rhombuses, crosses,

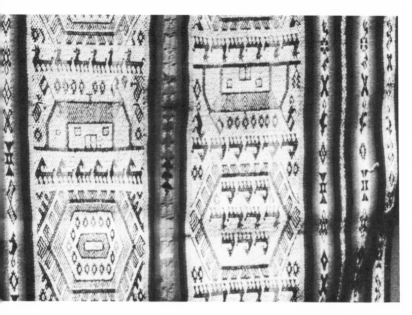

Paratíans are famous for the quality of their textile products. Literally dozens of motifs are included in the inventory of designs drawn upon by Paratían artisans. Each individual weaver selects a variety of motifs as embellishments for the cloth she is producing. The above sample exhibits several geometric forms as well as depictions of objects such as houses, flags, and alpacas. The union of two pieces of cloth is carefully disguised by embroidery, seen here between the two broad bands of figures.

arches, triangles, hexagons, pentagons, stripes, checkerboard patterns, and angles. Combining all these, a large number of other figures can be made, limited only by the imagination of the weaver. Women are very skilled in this art and are able to reproduce letters and phrases without knowing how to read or write. They can also imitate any pattern they might have in front of them. Geometric designs are the most common on both men's and women's garments.

Among the animal motifs, there are horses in a variety of stances, forms, and attitudes, standing as well as walking and running, with or without riders; viscachas, standing, walking, or sitting on their haunches; vicuñas at rest or in motion; deer, llamas, alpacas, dogs, rabbits, cats, *wallata,* ducks, and many kinds of birds. Pumas and foxes are also depicted.

Plant motifs are less common and are limited to what the people generally call *t'ika* (flowers). Among these are roses and daisies and isolated parts of plants, such as stems, leaves, and branches.

When the weavers portray human figures, they show horseback riders, men walking, women, human faces surrounded by lightning, dancing scenes, costumed men dancing with women, and children in front of houses, all in stylized form.

In general, each motif and figure has a specific name, such as *kili* (a geometric form), *rosa* (rose), *pato sacha* (duck shrub), *arko* (arch), *palka* (bifurcated), *qenqo* (zigzag), *awya* (dispersed), *kallawaya* (an Indian from a region in Bolivia), *mesa* (table), and many more.

Ponchos and *llijllas* are further embellished by the way in which they are finished. Both are made from two identical pieces of cloth that are sewn together. The seam has the appearance of embroidery because it is very fine and hides the union of the two pieces. This contrasts with the ends of each piece, where imperfections can be seen. The latter are caused by the large needles used in finishing a weaving.

From the Windy Cliffs to the Lowlands

When the head of a family feels that enough cloth goods have been woven, he takes a trip to the farmers' territory. There he will trade his textiles for the grains and tubers his family needs to subsist during the year.

On these commercial trips, ties are created with farmers in the "lowlands"—with groups along the shores of Lake Titicaca and adjacent areas in the same department of Puno, as well as with peasants in the neighboring departments of Arequipa, Moquegua, Tacna, and sometimes even Cuzco.

These trips, especially the longer ones to places several days away, involve work reserved for the men. Apprenticeship starts very early; even children of about seven or eight may

Each year the men of Paratía go on trading trips to agricultural communities at lower altitudes. Small groups of men and boys travel together during these commercial ventures, which may last as long as a month. The decision to set out on a trading trip is made when a family has accumulated a sufficient amount of trade goods. Broad-striped bags woven with alpaca thread and thick ropes braided from the wool of the llama are two of the pastoralists' manufactured items that are in strong demand among their peasant trading partners. Meat, hides, and fat are also important goods traded by the pastoralists. Barter is the primary mode of exchange between pastoralists and agriculturalists.

accompany their father in his regular travels through the southern Peruvian Andes. If for some reason a family has no adult males able to make the journey, its members will ask the help of close relatives, such as the brothers of a deceased husband, the brothers of the widow, the sons of the father's brothers, and, in extreme cases, of friends and neighbors. It is hard to find someone unwilling to lend assistance to such a family.

The commercial routes are covered on foot, the travelers proceeding between fifteen and twenty kilometers daily at the slow pace of the llamas, which, as we have said, are the most common beasts of burden among the Paratíans. Travelers may form close-knit groups on the basis of kinship, friendship, or residential neighborhood. Each group drives from fifteen to twenty llamas, although some caravans may number seventy, eighty, or even more llamas, for which additional helpers must be hired. They are sometimes paid in money, but more often in trade goods.

Since the men travel on a regular basis, they become accustomed to joining up with certain companions, and there are strong feelings of cooperation and solidarity within these groups. Many routes are covered only by particular groups, and nobody is in the habit of traveling alone because the risks would be too great. For each trip, the traders carry provisions, blankets, and even fuel for cooking, since some areas along the route are so arid that no kindling can be found. At the end of each day, the travelers camp at prearranged sites; these are sometimes caves, rocky overhangs, or ruined houses.

The greater part of the Paratíans' trade goods consists of woolen cloth, dried meat, fat, hides, and occasionally wool. But this is not all they trade; sometimes they serve as intermediaries. For example, they may go first to Pukará, in the province of Lampa, an area which produces ceramics. There they pick up clay goods which are transported to other regions in the same department of Puno or to neighboring departments, to exchange for agricultural products. On other occasions, they complement their cargo of woven goods with bags of edible clays (chaqo and phasalla), bringing them to Cabanillas, Pusi, and Capachica to barter for potatoes and perhaps a little barley and kañiwa.

Every year, the territory of these trading caravans gets a bit smaller. New roads and modern means of communication have encouraged others to take over part of the Paratíans' trade. For example, more than twenty years ago, Paratíans traveled as far as the Bolivian valley of Camacho, on the eastern side of Lake Titicaca (Map 3) taking a route that passes through the towns of Huancané and Rosaspata and close to Cojata. In Camacho, they bartered for oranges, coca, fresh corn in choclos (ears), and other products that grow in the

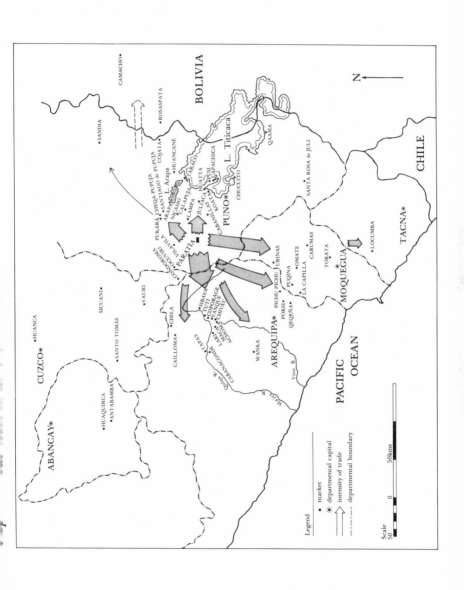

Legend

• market

◉ departmental capital

⬆ intensity of trade

–··– departmental boundary

Scale
50   0   50kms

warmer lowlands. Today these trips are no longer made and the Paratíans say "it is no longer worth going" because "it is too far." But another reason is that other traders now travel these areas in trucks. On the other hand, it is interesting to note that mechanization and modernization are also beginning to come to Paratía, since at least some herders travel by train and bus, hiring others to drive their llamas. There are, it seems, even those who have sent their llamas by truck.

Nonetheless, the routes we have just discussed have never been as important as the Arequipa and Moquegua routes, and probably for that reason they were abandoned with relative ease. There is a great commercial tradition linked to the valleys of Chivay and Cailloma in the department of Arequipa, as well as to the highlands of the basin of the Qolqa River, and from there to the fertile plains of Cabanaconde, the principal source of supply for wheat, barley, and corn, and to Yumina, Poksi, Wanka, Qeqeña, Lari, Maca, Achoma, and dozens of small settlements scattered throughout the sierras of Arequipa. When the traders go to Moquegua, they visit the immediate surroundings of Omate and the Ubinas volcano. On certain occasions they even go to the town of Moquegua itself, attracted by the quality of the apples, figs, and grapes that are grown there.

The basic mode of trade is barter. Although at times money is used, the main interest is in obtaining food, for which these people prefer to exchange their goods. The barter, about which we have little information, is carried out according to traditional exchange ratios. For example, it is customary to receive for a woven bag of a given volume an equal volume of ears of corn, and half its volume if it is exchanged for wheat or barley. For about a kilo of fat, a man will receive ten to twenty ears of corn or two or three kilos of barley or wheat.

In the department of Puno, the trade is concentrated in the area northwest of Lake Titicaca, the peninsula of Capachica, the edges of Lake Arapa, and the centers of Koata, Huatta, Santiago de Pupuja, Pukará, and many other farming settlements.

Few Paratíans travel the routes that go through the high zones of Yauri and Santo Tomás or through Sicuani in the

Llamas are used as beasts of burden on the trading trips. En route to the lowlands they carry bags filled with wool and other pastoral products. On the return home, they are loaded down with potatoes, barley, corn, and other agricultural produce needed by the pastoralists for their subsistence. Llamas can carry loads weighing thirty kilograms and cover a distance of twenty kilometers in a day.

department of Cuzco. It is said that sometimes Paratíans do go to Yauri or Santo Tomás for the well-known *chumbivilcano* horses, which are valued for their strength and beauty and are shown off by their owners as a sign of status and prestige.

Trading trips generally last a number of days. "Nearby" areas are reached on trips of approximately eight days' duration; those to "distant" places can easily occupy a month of traveling. The dry season is best suited for such travel since rain and snow would obviously hinder trading. During the rainy months the men devote themselves to other occupations such as shearing, overseeing the mating, caring for the herds of newborns, or simply enjoying themselves at the seemingly endless carnival fiestas.

Each community and each family has preferred trade routes which appear to be followed for generations. This regular contact with fixed groups of farmers has become institutionalized through bonds based on spiritual kinship (*compadrazgo*), with all the obligations and duties this type of relationship entails. Among the farmers' obligations are granting certain kinds of favors, such as in lodging; reserving their best products; and guaranteeing to provide them even in hard times when harvests are damaged by droughts, insect plagues, and so forth. Of course, there are also reciprocal benefits for the farmers. Trading occurs as part of a relationship between friends and acquaintances who may have known each other since childhood, when the herder accompanied his father to learn about the roads, people, and places he would eventually frequent on his own. Thus, these commercial transactions are not cold, calculating mercantile relationships but rather exchanges of goods between friends and ritual kinsmen. Each one needs the other, and their business is conducted in a friendly atmosphere, ending always with the expectation of another meeting. But these ties seldom go beyond the limits mentioned above, and never become strengthened through marriage. The natives neither know nor can remember any case in which a herder from Paratía married someone from the lowlands or decided to remain there to live. When Paratíans wish to migrate, they get on trucks in Lampa, or on the train at Santa Lucía, and go to Juliaca, Puno, Arequipa, and other distant places that are highly attractive for potential migrants.

Trading trips are the principal means by which Paratíans stock up on the annual supply of agricultural products. In addition to this commerce, there are minor commercial transactions for matches, alcohol, caramels, candles, cookies, sugar, beer, soft drinks, canned goods, thread, and other goods. In Paratía and other hamlets, there are small stores (*tiendas*) where these items can be purchased.

During the two annual religious festivals, many traveling merchants converge on Paratía from Santa Lucía, Lampa,

Cabanillas, and even Juliaca and Puno. They install their stands underneath awnings and sell articles that are impossible to find in the town on ordinary days—machine-made clothing, decorations for traditional clothing, kitchen utensils, and many other manufactured goods. These merchants stay for eight days or more, depending on the enthusiasm and number of people. Successful fiestas are signaled by a profusion of stands in the plaza and an extended stay. For these transactions, money is used, but the merchants also accept payment in wool, hides, fat, meat, and woven clothes.

Some of these peddlers are true specialists. They cover a large part of the department of Puno, including some bordering areas such as the "high" parts of Arequipa and Cuzco, taking their business from fair to fair and fiesta to fiesta.

Another group of specialized businessmen comes from Juliaca, Lampa, Huancané, Arequipa, and possibly Bolivia.* During certain times of the year, these visitors travel all of Paratía buying wool and sometimes the meat of lamoids and sheep. They also engage in the unlawful purchase of vicuña skins, thus serving as the indirect cause of the animal's impending extinction. With their methods of operation—giving monetary advances on which they charge high interest, using force and coercion to collect their debts—these buyers are a necessary and expected evil, but they are not popular in the area.

---

*It is interesting to note that according to the people of Paratía the traders who buy vicuña wool almost always are from Bolivia.

CHAPTER 4

ON THE QUESTION OF
PASTORALISM

OUR BRIEF ethnographic sketch of the herders of Paratía has shown that animal husbandry is their principal means of subsistence and the base on which they have built their economic system. We have collected some field data documenting the existence of these contemporary herding societies in the Andes, and can use these data as a basis to speculate about the antiquity of this type of economy in the area. The question is particularly important because it is widely assumed that pure pastoralism does not exist and perhaps never has existed in America. The common view is that the Andean economy, from the pre-Columbian epoch to the present time, has been mainly agricultural, based on the cultivation of the land.

We believe these assertions largely result from lack of information regarding vast regions of the Andean territory; in many areas few studies have been made and there is a scarcity of reliable ethnographic data. We think any contribution to this field of study should be welcomed—only with data in hand can we correct the inaccurate generalizations found even in important texts and introductory works on anthropology. Beals and Hoijer, and Hoebel, for example, who appear to use the same sources, offer the following general opinions:

All pastoral peoples are found in the Old World. . . . [Beals and Hoijer 1965:394]*

*The author used the Spanish editions of these works. However, I have quoted English editions of these texts in order to be as exact as

111

In the New World, only the Navahos became pastoralists—and then only in modern times with sheep acquired from the Spanish. [Hoebel 1972:267]

We could list many other references, but will limit ourselves to these remarks by Forde (1957:394), the author of a classic in anthropology:

Pastoralism as a dominant economy has been developed only in the Old World. It is true that domestic varieties of the native "camel" (guanaco and vicuña) of South America were reared in large herds in the higher civilization of the Andean plateaux, but live stock was there an auxiliary and integral part of a developed agricultural and sedentary civilization. The flesh of the llama (the domesticated guanaco) was eaten to a certain extent, but this animal served mainly to carry burdens in large trains, while the alpaca (the domesticated vicuña) was kept only for its wool. No autonomous or semi-independent communities of herders were found either within or beyond the orbit of the native Peruvian civilization. The only truly pastoral people of the New World are the Navajo of the North American Southwest, and their present economy has been developed subsequent to and consequent on the Spanish introduction of sheep and horses, already completely domesticated and associated with fixed patterns or uses.

It is clear, then, that our information on Paratía has both theoretical and practical value for the study of the entire central Andes. Despite its interest, this region has been examined only in relation to "intensive agriculture" or as an "area of agrarian economy." Perhaps in part because the herders live more than four thousand meters above sea level, they have been largely ignored. We strongly believe that this omission ought now to be taken into consideration.

To clarify our concepts and avoid confusion, it is worth stating that a culture may be considered pastoral even though it does not include every possible use of animals. The African examples of this principle are clear and worth noting, as Forde (1957:401) states so well:

possible. It should be pointed out that later editions of these works made essentially the same claims, in some instances with no changes in the wording. [Trans.]

The known uses to which domestic animals can be put by pastoral peoples are, briefly, first: the consumption of the meat, and occasionally the blood, and the use of the hides; to this extent they are merely tame "game"; second, the use of hair and wool as a textile or felting material; third, the milking of the females, thus providing a source of food which does not necessitate the slaughter of the beasts and is unknown to food-gatherers and the lower cultivators, except of course in hybrid cultures such as are found in south-eastern Africa; fourth, the conversion of the milk into dairy products which can be conserved for considerable periods; fifth, the use of the animals as beasts of burden or even of draught; sixth, the riding of animals. To us all these well-known practices may appear obvious, but it is important to realize that many pastoralists are completely unaware of some or all of them excepting only the first.

It would be wise to add to this list the not so easily discounted use of dung as fuel. This product is particularly important at altitudes above four thousand meters where it is very difficult to find sources of firewood, and where other combustible resources, such as charcoal, may not be available. Of the six activities Forde presents (which in our opinion do not exclude the Andean case), two are common in Paratía and one is seen on certain occasions. Paratíans use the alpacas' wool for weaving and rely on the physical strength of the llamas as beasts of burden; they also use the meat, blood, and skins of the animals, and preserve the dung for fuel.

The *Regional Development Plan for Southern Peru* (Plan Regional 1959), a bibliographical source cited before, contains a very interesting reference to this subject. It is found in the results of a survey of property conducted in Paratía:

Number of properties	71
Total area (in hectares)	27,095
Cultivated area (hectares)	1
Noncultivated arable area (hectares)	6
Pasturelands (hectares)	27,088
Number of animals	37,534
Properties without data but considered in the sample	3

Seventy-one properties, with a total of 27,095 hectares, contain 27,088 hectares in pasturelands. It is logical to suppose that alpacas are grazed on these lands, although this unfortunately is not indicated by the source. A hectare dedicated to "cultivation" raises questions, but we believe this refers to the small plots used in experiments with grasses on some of the mestizo haciendas. But even if this hectare involved true cultivation, such a small amount would not transform the Paratíans into farmers, since it would represent only 0.0037 percent of the total acreage considered in the sample, a statistically insignificant percentage. Besides, the survey does not specify to whom the hectare belongs. It might refer to experimental plots on properties near the districts of Lampa, Santa Lucía, or Pukará, or other neighboring districts, where incipient and limited potato cultivation does in fact exist.

But just as the possession of three sheep and one cow by a native farmer in the Vilcanota Valley of Cuzco does not turn him into a herder, so one cultivated parcel of land among the thousands dedicated to pasturing does not turn an alpaca herder into a farmer. In ethnological literature, classic and known examples of pastoral peoples include the Tungus, the Kazak, the Kirghiz, the Masai, the Tiv, and the Nuer, to name only a few. Even among some of these tribes it is possible to find evidence of agriculture, and this does not change their pastoral orientation. On this question we will again cite Forde (1957:343):

Although the Kazak are essentially pastoralists, agricultural products are produced on a small scale. Whenever physical conditions suitable for the diversion of river water offer opportunities for irrigation, water channels and embanked plots are laid out for millet, wheat and rye and, in the far south, for rice. Much of this cultivation is undertaken by dependent peasants who are not Kazaks, and in former times slaves from the oasis settlements were used. But small groups of true Kazaks are also found engaged in cultivation and remain at work in the fields from spring to autumn. These are mostly poor families with little or no livestock of their own, who depend for their livelihood on service to richer families who provi them with meat and milk products.*

---

*See also Gulliver (1968a:264–265).

Kazak agriculture is technically similar to that of the oases of central and south-western Asia, although the standard of cultivation is often much lower.

The existence of pastoral groups in the central Andes, and particularly in the south of Peru, seems to be more prevalent than one might think at first sight. We have evidence that there are other pastoralists within the department of Puno in the region around Santa Rosa de Juli, in the province of Chucuito, and in the districts of Ocuviri and Vilavila in the province of Lampa. They are also found in the so-called "highlands" of the province of Canchis and in the district of Condoroma in the province of Espinar, both areas in the department of Cuzco. Our information also suggests that there are pastoral groups in Huaquirca, a district in the province of Antabamba in the department of Apurímac. The reports indicate that the natives in this area graze alpacas in the high zones and sheep, cattle, and horses at lower elevations, although the herds of these European species are small and not as important as the alpacas. Agricultural products are obtained in exchange for tending and pasturing the farmers' cattle or through trade. The homes of the herders closest to Huaquirca are two kilometers from the central village and the farthest are up to a day away on horseback, about thirty kilometers (Juvenal Casaverde, personal communication).

Finally, there are more tangible and concrete data in the ethnological study by Nachtigall (1966), showing the presence of a group of pastoralists in the cordillera of the department of Moquegua along the salt flats of Pichu Pichu. We believe this area is culturally linked with the Altiplano and belongs only in an administrative sense to Moquegua. Alpaca herding also caught the attention of Nachtigall, and his description is quite valuable.*

In the study of the Andean economy, we believe it is important to take into consideration that, for some groups, re-

---

*This publication was made available to us by Dr. John V. Murra when this book was being prepared.

sources other than those provided by agriculture are of the greatest significance. We can begin to increase our understanding of the indigenous economy in the contemporary Andes if we broaden our range of study. Consider, for example, the groups living on the shores of Lake Titicaca, subsisting on what they obtain through fishing and the gathering of totora reeds, which, among other things, permit them to fatten livestock for later sale in the regional fairs and markets. With the money from this trade they then acquire agricultural products. When groups like this practice agriculture it is on such a reduced scale that it sometimes has a merely supplementary character; certainly in no case is it the main source of income. One ethnological work illustrates this situation among the group called the Uru of Qaama, in the district of Pomata, department of Puno (Cordero 1966).

The case of the community of Cheqa-Pupuja should also be mentioned, since it is very similar to dozens of other communities in that region. Located in the district of José Domingo Choqewanka, province of Azángaro, also in Puno, Cheqa-Pupuja is famous for its ceramic figures known as "Pukará bulls." The people of this community have small agricultural plots on which they raise potatoes, *oka, isaño,* and *kinuwa,* among other things. However, the bulk of the local economy is based on the production and marketing of ceramics, which permit the people to trade for vegetable products. These resources are supplemented with the income from meager flocks that provide wool to weave *bayeta,* from which the people make their own clothing (Cátedra de Investigación de Folklore 1966). Another example of this sort of economy is Rajchi in Canchis, Cuzco, where the people devote themselves to making ceramics and fattening their cattle, and only in a lesser degree to agriculture, although farming is admittedly of greater importance here than in the Puno communities.

We turn now to another point raised at the beginning of this chapter. How ancient is this type of pastoralism? Although there is not yet enough historical information to answer this question definitively, there are three possibilities worthy of consideration:

(a) that pastoralism has a long tradition extending back to pre-Hispanic times;

(b) that the contemporary pastoral groups are the descendants of farmers who were displaced towards higher locations, less favorable for agriculture, by the Spanish invaders; to survive in these "refuge regions," they had to adopt animal husbandry;

(c) that these groups are the remnants of specialized pastoralists who tended the herds of an agricultural society, and that the ties binding them to the farmers were severed because of the sudden invasion of the Europeans. They remained in the same place and became pastoral peoples, providing themselves with the necessary agricultural products through trade.

Many other possibilities could be suggested, but all of them would require lengthy historical studies which we have not been able to carry out, although we hope this can be done in the future. But it is possible to argue tentatively that the pastoral way of life originated in pre-Columbian times. If we take into account the fact that the habitat has not undergone major changes in the last millennium—the known changes occurred two thousand years ago—and the fact noted on page 88 in the quotation by Murra, that the Altiplano was the area where alpacas were first domesticated, we might suppose that there were people even then whose lives were dedicated exclusively to herding and who obtained agricultural products such as corn through trade with lowland farmers, to whom they provided wool, meat, hides, and textiles. Without resorting to archeological sources, since that would take us further than we wish to go at present, we know that cloth made of alpaca wool has been found on the coast and that such cloth can be dated to periods before the Incas, and finally that the wool probably was acquired through commerce. This presumption, combined with the ubiquitous presence of pre-Columbian burial sites throughout the barren expanses of the Altiplano, leads us to conclude that herders could have existed there during those times.

Our decision not to venture too far beyond the sphere of ethnography does not prevent us from quoting some chroniclers who observed the great population density and numbers of "animals of the earth" found in the Altiplano. Even though they do not provide precise information about pure pastoralism, these sources give clues that allow us to hypothesize its existence. Cieza (1941:286–287) says:

From the town of Chicuana, which belongs to this province of the Canas, to Ayaviri there are fifteen leagues. In this area there are some settlements of Canas and many plains, and large pampas quite suitable for raising cattle, although the extreme coldness of the region hinders it; the multitude of grasses growing there does not benefit anything except the guanacos and vicuñas.

Later (p. 290) he adds:

So that, although in all Collao corn is neither gathered nor planted, the native people . . . do not lack for it because they never stop bringing loads of corn, coca, and fruits of all kinds.

Cobo (1956:365–366) also tells us:

God created the llamas in these cold lands for the good of their inhabitants, who without these cattle would spend their lives with great difficulty since these are very barren lands where cotton for clothing cannot be obtained, as in the warm lands, and to buy it from outside for so many people would be impossible; nor do they cultivate many fruit trees or vegetables. Therefore, the Giver of all goods, God Our Lord, made up for the barren *punas* and uninhabitable plains of the sierras by creating in them so many of these tame animals that their number could not be estimated because there were so many, making up all the wealth of the highland Indians. They dressed in the wool and made footwear from the skins; they did not wear anything on their bodies except what they obtained from their llamas. They sustained themselves with the meat, and used them as beasts to take and bring their loads by drayage and transport. With the meat and the clothing they made from them, they bought and traded in the valleys and hot lands for what they lacked, such goods as *ají*, fish, corn, coca, fruits, and everything else they needed. In the *yunga* lands, the dwellers lacked meat, because these cattle did not exist there, and they did not have another tamed animal to supply this need until cattle from Spain were brought, which are now abundant everywhere.

As we can see, the herds were numerous, but in order to subsist and vary their diet the people needed agricultural products, and these were obtained through trade with the valleys and other lands. "Meat" and "the clothing they made from them," that is to say, their textiles, were given in exchange. Animal husbandry, weaving, and trade were the major productive activities then, just as they are today among the group we have studied.

The theories presented in this chapter cannot be confirmed or rejected until more information has been gathered. In the meantime, the herders of the *ayllus* of Paratía continue to tend their alpacas, weaving their cloth and traveling over the routes that their fathers and their fathers' fathers have followed for generations, driving trains of llamas loaded with textiles and animal products. But for how long? We do not know. This question could only be answered by the Spirit of the Windy Cliffs, *Apu Wayra Qaqa,* and the Spirit of Philinko, *Apu Philinko.*

BIBLIOGRAPHY

Aguirre Beltrán, Gonzalo
1967 *Regiones de refugio*. Ediciones Especiales, 46. Mexico City: Instituto Indigenista Interamericano.
Baca Mendoza, Oswaldo, Efraín Morote Best, Oscar Núñez del Prado, and Josafat Roel Pineda
1954 *Sistema único de escritura para las lenguas quechua y aymara*. Universidad Nacional del Cuzco. Cuzco: Ed. Garcilaso.
Beals, Ralph, and Harry Hoijer
1965 *An Introduction to Anthropology* [1953]. 3rd Edition. New York: Macmillan.
Bertonio, Ludovico
1879 *Vocabulario de la lengua aymara* [1612]. 2nd Edition. Facsimile. Leipzig: Julio Platzmann.
Bourricaud, François
1954 "Algunas características originales de la cultura mestiza en el Perú contemporáneo," *Revista del Museo Nacional* (Lima), 23:162–173.
1963 "Castas y clases en Puno," *Revista del Museo Nacional* (Lima), 33:308–321.
1967 *Cambios en Puno*. Ediciones Especiales, 48. Mexico City: Instituto Indigenista Interamericano.
Cátedra de Investigación de Folklore. Director: Demetrio Roca. Participants: Yemira Nájar; Teresa Zúñiga; Jorge A. Flores-Ochoa; Aurelio Carmona Cruz; Leandro Zans Candia; and Walter Tapia Bueno. Editing and final revision: Demetrio Roca and Jorge Flores-Ochoa.
1966 "El torito de Pukara (cerámica tradicional de Ch'eqa Pupuja)," *Folklore: revista de cultura tradicional* (Cuzco), 1(1):103–146.
Choy, Emilio
1960 "La revolución neolítica en los orígenes de la civilización americana," in *Antiguo Perú: éspacio tiempo*, pp. 149–197. Lima: Mejía Baca.

Cieza de León, Pedro
1941   *La crónica del Perú* [1550]. Madrid: Espasa Calpe.
Cobo, Bernabé
1956   *Historía del Nuevo Mundo* [1653]. Madrid: Biblioteca de Autores Españoles.
Cordero Eduardo, Ariel
1966   *Los uros de Qaama.* Manuscript. Departamento de Antropología, Universidad Nacional del Cuzco, Cuzco.
CORPUNO
1964   "Separata del VI Censo Nacional de Población." Mimeographed. Puno.
Cuentas, E.
1956   "Estampas puneñas: la fiesta de San Pedro en Icho," *Revista del Instituto Americano de Arte de Puno* (El Deber, Puno), 5:26–30.
Downs, James
1964   *Animal Husbandry in Navajo Society and Culture.* University of California Publications in Anthropology, Volume 1. Berkeley and Los Angeles: University of California Press.
Evans-Pritchard, E. E.
1941   "The Nuer of the Southern Sudan," in *African Political Systems,* M. Fortes and E. E. Evans-Pritchard, eds., pp. 272–296. International Institute of African Language and Culture. London: Oxford University Press.
Flores-Ochoa, Jorge A.
1964   "Pastores del Ande sur-peruano," *Revista de la Universidad Técnica del Altiplano* (Puno) 2:231–238. Cuzco: Rozas.
1966   "El ayarachi," *Folklore: revista de cultura tradicional* (Cuzco), 1(1):67–82.
Forde, C. Daryll
1957   *Habitat, Economy and Society: A Geographical Introduction to Ethnology* [1934]. London: Methuen.
Gilmore, Raymond
1950   "Fauna and Ethnozoology of South America," in *Handbook of South American Indians,* Vol. 6, J. Steward, ed., pp. 345–464. Bureau of American Ethnology Bulletin 143. Washington: Smithsonian Institution.
Gulliver, P. H.
1968a   "The Jie of Uganda," in *Man in Adaptation: The Cultural Present,* Yehudi Cohen, ed., pp. 262–284. Chicago: Aldine.
1968b   "The Turkana," in *Man in Adaptation: The Cultural Present,* Yehudi Cohen, ed., pp. 284–299. Chicago: Aldine.
Herrera, Fortunato L.
1918   "Flora apurimensis," *Revista universitaria órgano de la Universidad del Cuzco,* 7(24–25):75–85.

1921   *Contribuciones a la flora del departamento del Cuzco.* Cuzco: Rozas.

1934   *Catálogo alfabético de los nombres de las plantas que existen en el Perú.* Lima: Universidad Nacional Mayor de San Marcos.

Hoebel, E. Adamson
1972   *Anthropology: The Study of Man* [1949]. 4th Edition. New York: McGraw-Hill.

Jacobs, Melville, and Bernhard Stern
1964   *General Anthropology.* New York: Barnes and Noble.

Mangin, William P.
1964   "Estratificación social en la Callejón de Huaylas," in *Estudios sobre la cultura actual del Perú,* pp. 16–36. Lima: Universidad Nacional Mayor de San Marcos.

Marín, Felipe
1961   "Panorama fitogeográfico del Perú," *Revista universitaria: órgano de la Universidad Nacional de San Antonio Abad del Cuzco* (Cuzco), 1(120):9–66.

Mishkin, Bernard
1946   "The Contemporary Quechua," in *Handbook of South American Indians,* Vol. 2, J. Steward, ed., pp. 501–573. Bureau of American Ethnology Bulletin 143. Washington: Smithsonian Institution.

Moro, Manuel
1964   "Las alpacas," *Cultura y pueblo* (Publicación de la Comisión Nacional de Cultura, Lima), 1(4):33–34.

Murra, John V.
1964   "Rebaños y pastores en la economía del Tahuantinsuyo," *Revista peruana de cultura* (Lima), 2:76–77.

Nachtigall, Horst
1966   *Indianische Fischer, Feldbauer, undV iehzuchter: Beiträge zur Peruanischen Volkerkunde.* Berlin: Dietrich Reimer.

Núñez del Prado Castro, Oscar
1953   *Problemas antropológicos del área andina.* Cuzco: Rozas.

Plan Regional
1959   *Plan regional para el desarrollo del sur del Perú.* Vols. I, IV, V, XII, XXII, XXIV, XXVI. Multigraphed. Lima.

Poma de Ayala, Phelipe Guamán
1956   *El primer nueva coronica y buen gobierno* [1587–1615]. Interpretada por Luis F. Bustíos Gálvez. Lima: Ministerio de Guerra.

Pulgar Vidal, Javier
1946   *Historía y geografía del Perú: las ocho regiones naturales del Perú.* Lima: Universidad Nacional Mayor de San Marcos.

Rowe, John Howland
1946   "Inca Culture at the Time of the Spanish Conquest," in

Handbook of South American Indians, Vol. 2, J. Steward, ed., pp. 183–331. Bureau of American Ethnology Bulletin 143. Washington: Smithsonian Institution.

Sanmartí, Primitivo
1905   *Los pueblos del Perú.* Lima: San Pedro.
Sauer, Carl
1950   "Geography and Plant and Animal Resources," in *Handbook of South American Indians*, Vol. 6, J. Steward, ed., pp. 319–344. Bureau of American Ethnology Bulletin 143. Washington: Smithsonian Institution.
Towle, Margaret A.
1961   *The Ethnobotany of Pre-Columbian Peru.* Chicago: Aldine.
Troll, Carlos
1958   "Las culturas superiores andinas y el medio geográfico," *Revista del Instituto de Geografía* (Lima), 5.
Valcárcel, Luis E.
1964a   *Ruta cultural del Perú* [1945]. Lima: Ediciones Nuevo Mundo.
1964b   *Etnohistoria del Perú antiguo: historia del Perú (Incas)* [1958]. Lima: Universidad Nacional Mayor de San Marcos.
Winick, Charles
1961   *Dictionary of Anthropology.* New Jersey: Littlefield-Adams.

1 2 3 4 5 6 7 8 9 10 11 12 13   88 87 86 85 84 83 82 81 80 79